D1616015

THOROUGHBRED

THOROUGHBRED

BURTON L. SPILLER
AUTHOR OF "GROUSE FEATHERS"

Illustrated by Lynn Bogue Hunt

THE PREMIER COLLECTION

The Premier Press
Camden, South Carolina
1993

Three Thousand copies of
THOROUGHBRED
have been printed for
The Premier Collection.
This book is number

2522

The special contents of this edition have been produced for
The Premier Collection and are copyright1993 by The Premier Press.
Premier Press Advisory Board: John Culler, Chairman;
Thomas W. Culler; James A. Casada, Ph.D.; Sheldon M. Spindel.
This volume designed by Laurie Brownell McIntosh.
Printed in the United States of America.

TO

M. M. M.

FOREWORD

Burton Lowell Spiller (1886-1973) belonged to a generation of outdoor scribes which gave us a splendid legacy of sporting literature. His contemporaries or near contemporaries included individuals such as Harold Sheldon, Havilah Babcock, Archibald Rutledge, Nash Buckingham, and others. In company with men of their ilk, Spiller brought delight, not to mention literary light, to the dens of countless sportsmen. Better still, as was true of the other writers just mentioned, his writing had about it a timelessness, an enduring quality, which still enchants today as it did in yesteryear.

Burton L. Spiller was born on December 21, 1886 in Portland, Maine. The son of a farmer, he grew up with a close bond to the good earth. He hunted in and roamed through the woods around his boyhood home in what must have been in many senses an idyllic childhood, and the experiences of these years served him well once he began to take pen to paper. His roots are of considerable interest, because he enjoyed none of the silver spoon upbringing many others of his generation who wrote on sport were privileged to know. Spiller's education was limited to what the public schools of the day could provide, but in the school of the outdoors, where there is no graduation day, he was a keen lifelong student.

According to George Bird Evans, who offers short profiles of Spiller in *Men Who Shot* and *George Bird Evans Introduces* (the pieces are essentially the same), this staunch son of the New England soil was something of a jack-of-all-trades. For a time he pursued the hot, demanding work which is a blacksmith's lot; he raised gladioli bulbs for the commercial market; and he worked for a few years in the Portsmouth Naval Yard. Yet for all that these career pursuits were distinctly plebian, when it came to sport and writing thereon Spiller's instincts were unquestionably patrician. This was especially true when it came to grouse hunting, which was Spiller's consuming sporting passion, but the pages of the present work also echo that sense for and savoring of that elusive essence we call "quality." In other words, his humble background notwithstanding, as a sportsman and a writer Spiller merited the description "thoroughbred" he chose as the title for the volume presently being reprinted.

Spiller had already done a fair amount of writing for major outdoor magazines when his first book appeared, but it was the publication of that volume, *Grouse Feathers*, which really heralded his arrival as a sporting scribe of national note. Published in 1935 by Eugene Virginius Connett's famed Derrydale Press, *Grouse Feathers* was the first of four volumes by Spiller to appear under that imprint in as many years. This output can only be viewed as a prodigious feat of literary productivity. The volume reprinted here, *Thoroughbred,* was published in 1936, followed in rapid-fire order by *Firelight* (1937) and *More Grouse Feathers* (1938).

Then came a lengthy hiatus in books prior to the issue of *Drummer in the Woods,* a grouse hunting classic, in 1962. Here again we see evidence of Connett's fine editorial eye and wide-ranging contacts, because the doyen of the Derrydales went to work for Van Nostrand, which published *Drummer in the Woods,* after the closure of his own press during World War II. Spiller's final book, *Fishin' Around,* was published posthumously by Winchester Pre~s in 1974. He had died in May of the previous year, aged 86, at his East Rochester, New Hampshire home.

Despite the interlude of almost a quarter century between the publication of his last Derrydale and *Drummer in the Woods,* which many consider to be the finest of Spiller's sextet of books, Spiller by no means abandoned his literary labors. Examine, for example, the pages of *Field & Stream* in the 1940s and 1950s. There you will find Spiller's byline, on a fairly regular basis, with most of his pieces being on some aspect of upland game hunting.

It was during the heyday of the Derrydale Press, however, that Spiller was at the peak of his powers and productivity. Along with Nash Buckingham, H. G. Pickering, Colonel Harold Sheldon, and Edmund Ware Smith, he was one of the the most active authors in Connett's stable of contributors. In that regard, there is little question that the repeat appearances of all these writers stemmed from the same explanation—Connett knew quality when he saw it.

FOREWORD

Certainly such was the case with Spiller. Today all of his books, with the possible exception of *Fishin' Around*, are considered by sporting bibliophiles to be classics. Spiller has become almost a cult figure among grouse hunters and is frequently described as "the poet laureate of grouse shooting." As the present work readily suggests though, Spiller's abilities transcended the romance of remote coverts and the pursuit of grouse. He had a special knack for capturing the allure of the outdoors with verve and vitality, and to read any of his books is to know vicarious sporting pleasure of the sort which suggest that currently fashionable audiovisual productions will never replace the joys of armchair adventure.

For some strange reason, the present volume is less well known than most of Spiller's other books. Yet it was accorded an enthusiastic reception when it appeared. Reviewers were uniform in their praise for *Thoroughbred*. For example, coverage in the *Boston Transcript* of May 29, 1936, says that "Mr. Spiller draws with infinite care a series of charming portraits of field trials and bird dogs and other animals, and surrounds them with real and frequently 'thoroughbred' people." Perry Hutchison, writing in the *New York Times*, states "Mr. Spiller's varied tales are of such good stuff, . . . simply and so genuinely told." Hutchison went on to comment that "this limited edition is of the finest; the binding is handsome in the extreme and the illustrations by Lynn Bogue Hunt are fascinatingly executed."

As I lovingly handle my personal copy of the Derrydale original, I heartily heartily with the reviewers' thoughts on both the

FOREWORD

quality of Spiller's writing and the physical appearance the Derrydale volume offered. A handsome pointer, outlined in gold, adorns the front cover, and the gold lettering on the spine and front stands out in pleasing fashion against the deep blue cloth. It is the eight stories of which *Thoroughbred* is comprised, however, which constitute its most enduring quality.

To my knowledge the book has not previously been reprinted, and the original is today quite rare. It cost $10 (a lot of money in the midst of the Great Depression) as a Derrydale, and it was limited to a printing of 950 copies. Today fine copies of the book are worth somewhere in the $250-$300 range, and ones with the original dust jacket are valued appreciably higher.

With this volume you can add *Thoroughbred* to your shelves and know that it bespeaks the kind of quality the author and original publisher cherished. More than that, its pages will take you down darkening avenues into a sporting past we have, sadly, now largely lost. You will be reminded that fine outdoors literature can and often does focus on simple subjects, and the dog stories offered here are truly of top quality. Take these pieces individually or as a collection—either way, you have an armchair or bedside companion to treasure.

JIM CASADA
ROCK HILL, SOUTH CAROLINA
SEPTEMBER 1, 1993

CONTENTS

ILLUSTRATIONS

THE SABLE KING

WITH his hand upraised to snap the patent lock on Number 17 yard, Jim McElwood paused and listened intently.

From the little hut in the center of the twenty foot pen came faint whimperings and subdued mewings, not unlike the cry of very young kittens. McElwood deposited the basket of chopped meat on the ground and leaned forward as he tried to separate the sounds into their component parts, and guess thereby at the number of the new arrivals.

Be it known that Labrador Queen VII, winner of firsts at each of the numerous shows in which she had been entered, accredited by fanciers, furriers and sportsmen throughout the land with the distinction of being the most perfect silver black fox in existence, had whelped during the night. The whimperings were the hunger cries of her offspring, crawling blindly about her beautiful body, taking their first lesson from Mother Nature in the rugged school of life.

"Sure, 'tis a whoppin' litter," McElwood whispered. "Will ye hear that feller growl, now? It's a buster he is, I'm thinkin'. It's his meal ticket he has between his paws, and he's goin' to hang on to it in spite of hell—and high water. It's lookin' at 'em I would be in a minute if it wa'n't against the rules to disturb her. She might take it into her head to kill 'em all. Well, Queen, it's nothin' you get to eat till night, but you'll be gettin' a plenty then."

Picking up the basket he tiptoed softly away and stopped at the next yard. Opening the gate he stepped within the enclosure. A magnificent black male fox advanced daintily to meet him, pointed ears erect and delicate nostrils sniffing for a hint as to the contents of the basket. McElwood deposited the allotted portion of meat in the pan and stood back while Labrador King ate. "A beautiful boy ye are," he crooned, "and it's a happy one ye ought to be, seein' as how you're a father several times over this mornin'. It's a shame ye can't go in and see the missus and the kids for a few minutes, but rules is rules, me boy. You, bein' a heathen, might decide to gobble up about five thousand dollars' worth of tender young meat for your breakfast so, father or no father, here ye stay in your own pen."

Labrador King paid no attention to the words but after the Irishman had left him he listened to the sounds emanating from the neighboring hut. McElwood was right. It was a "whoppin' litter." The fluffy balls of rusty black squirmed and struggled fretfully about their recumbent mother and snarled puny battle cries as they were pushed away by others of the family.

But one pup neither fretted nor snarled. A full third

larger than any of the others he had already secured the best position, and no amount of pushing by his brothers and sisters could move him from it. To him life was already a serious business and now, with ears flattened back, forepaws diligently kneading the warm breast, his little jaws steadily drew forth the fluid that meant life itself.

Not only in size did he differ from the others, but in color as well. Their coats were a dull, lifeless black that, while giving promise of the beautiful things they might become, yet lacked beauty in themselves. His fur glistened even in the semidarkness of the hut. It was a rich, luminous black with all the sheen and luster of the fur seal combined with the velvety softness of the sable. This was enhanced and accentuated by a mere pin point of white at the very tip of each hair. He was a thing of beauty even at birth.

McElwood had spent a long apprenticeship in black-fox farming. In the four years he had spent in charge of the Maine State Fox Farms he had seen hundreds of pups, yet he gasped in surprise at the sheer beauty of this animal when, three days later, while Labrador Queen had slipped out into the yard for her double portion of meat, he had cautiously lifted the hinged cover of the hut and peeped in at the litter.

"It's a fine lookin' pup ye are, me boy, and a credit to the old folks," he crooned. "Not that they're carin' a cuss whether it's red, white or blue that ye are, bein' uneducated as to the merits of the primal colors. Sure, and I'm tele-phonin' the directors this very mornin' to come up and have a look at ye."

The next day they came: sleek, well-groomed men of affairs. They enthused over the litter and especially over the sable pup.

"A freak," they pronounced him, "but one that might well become the progenitor of a new and valuable strain. Give him every attention," they told McElwood, "even if it becomes necessary to sacrifice one or two of the others in order that he may receive proper nourishment."

"Sure, it's little need ye have to worry about him," the Irishman answered. "That boy has a seat at the head of the table and stays wid it from soup to nuts every meal and to the divil wid the expense. Look at the coat of him, will ye? Look at the coat of him, for all the world like a black setter trailin' a pheasant through a frosty brier patch. When he's a year old ye can name your price for him—and get it, too."

Which prediction came nearer to being the truth than are many prophecies. The following autumn, in company with others, the sable pup was exhibited at many New Eng-land fairs and drew the attention of fox fanciers throughout the whole country. "Maine's Sable King," they called him, and a king he was through every fiber of his magnificent body. With all the grace and beauty of the wild, yet with none of its furtive shrinking, he faced the ever-changing throng before him, clear eyed and calm, giving glance for glance with a dignity that made him regal.

Thousands of women, passing by the cages that contained his brothers and sisters, accorded them a brief glance, but they stopped involuntarily before the Sable King. Invariably their eyes filled with tears and as invariably they made the same exclamation: "Oh! The poor, dear thing."

But the Sable King heeded them not. Despite the fact that behind him were seven generations of ancestors that had been raised in captivity, he was as much a creature of the wild as though his nostrils had never scented man. Healthy, well fed and physically content, there had come to him from other generations the heritage of the open spaces. When the north wind blew he showed signs of restlessness. With head held high, ears pointed forward and sharp nose outthrust, his delicate nostrils drew in the crisp air in long, wistful inhalations.

Then, after a time, he would curl up in a ball and lie unmoving, his somnolent eyes opening occasionally to gaze, unwinking, toward that far, unknown country of his dreams. And, of all those that saw him thus, only the Irishman understood.

"Sure, boy, it's seein' the snow-covered hills of the

North, ye are, and feelin' the wind sweep down across the barrens while the trees snap and bend to the breath of it; while I'm thinkin' of a little cabin in the County of Cork with a bit of a pig rootin' round it and the chickens and the geese not mindin' at all which side of the door-sill they're standin' on. There's green shamrock on the hills and lakes a-gleamin' in the sun down in the valleys. Ah, me boy, home's where the heart is, and you and me's a divil of a long ways from that place, I'm thinkin'!"

Then the King would turn his head majestically and look into the man's face. Creatures apart were they by every tradition, by the hundreds of years of enmity in which man was the hunter and the other the quarry. Despite the inbred instinct of the wild that taught its children that the scent of man was the harbinger of death, there yet existed between them an indefinable, intangible bond. Neither recognized it or admitted it even to himself yet each was aware of its existence and, as time went on, the bond grew stronger.

Of the seventy-two foxes in the yards at the farm the Sable King was the least domesticated and yet it was he alone that McElwood dared handle with impunity. The lightninglike fangs of the others had left many livid scars on the knotted hands that had inadvertently strayed too near their shrinking bodies but the King had never yet snarled fear or anger at the hand that fed him.

Nevertheless the King had one mortal enemy. One of the incumbrances wished on the farm by its zealous directors was a big, brindle brute of a dog whose ancestry, though known, would have found little favor in the eyes of a dog lover. His father was a cross between a timid pointer and a big, Southern hound that had been sold North, because of his varmint-hunting proclivities, making a detestable mongrel with the dull, heavy head of the hound and the slim, graceful body of the pointer mother. He, in turn, had mated with an outlaw shepherd who had so far forgotten the sovereign power of man that she made a practice of killing his sheep at regular intervals.

There could be but one possible outcome of such a mating, and this dog was the exemplification of it. A full fifty-five pounds in weight and every ounce concealing a different streak of meanness, he tried the very soul of the Irishman whose assistant he was supposed to be.

No man could look at the dog without an open sneer and this had gradually shown its effect on his already vile disposition. Man he hated, collectively and individually and, had it not been for the yellow in him that was considerably more than a streak, he would have been a real menace to the human race.

He had cultivated a snarl that was blood-curdling and a ferocious bark that could be heard for miles. Using these at the slightest provocation, he had created his sole recommendation for the position he now held. If hideous threats of mayhem, decapitation and other equally unpleasant operations would frighten off midnight marauders, then this particular fox farm was amply protected.

"Satan" was the name the fat director had given him when he had brought him, securely muzzled, to the farm and given him into the Irishman's charge.

"Satan, is it?" queried the irate McElwood. "Sure it's an appropriate name you have given him. He looks like hell. And what breed do you call it?"

The fat man chuckled. "It is a—er—recent importation we have made as an additional insurance on our investment," he announced. "He is a new strain."

"That's what I'm thinkin'. A new strain on me that's already got more than I can stand. It's a strain on the nerves just to look at him. Take the divil back to his home."

Again the director laughed. He was too good natured to take exception to the implied suggestion, but he was obdurate and, in the end, Satan stayed.

Immediately he became the terror of the farm, and the half-tamed creatures that inhabited it fled in wild alarm at the sound of that bellowing roar. Even the King trembled, but he did not run. He alone detected the false note in that mighty volume of sound.

Satan might indeed be a demon to the smaller and weaker creatures but he was a mongrel cur and his was a mongrel's cowardly heart. In the wilds, when that craven note entered into the voice of one of Nature's children, whether that creature were the tiniest mole burrowing in darkness below the grass roots, or the biggest of bears treading heavily above him, it meant death. Nature had no place for a weakling. Always there waited some valiant-hearted enemy, listening for that craven note and, when it came, the end was swift and certain. For only thus, by the prompt elimination of the weakling, could the race survive.

The meeting between the dog and the King was memorable in that it caused an incident which neither ever forgot, nor did McElwood, who witnessed it.

On the second day of his stay at the farm, Satan entered the main inclosure, a nine foot, woven wire fence that encircled the smaller yards. As he trotted belligerently down the lanes between these individual yards he was quick to note that the inmates frenziedly rushed into the safe shelter of their huts at sight of his awesome form, and his cowardly heart thrilled at the sight. When one old dog fox, nearly domesticated, hesitated for a moment, he flung himself bodily against the restraining wires and emitted a blood-curdling roar. Its effect was instantaneous and every fox, save one, fled precipitately.

[9]

That one exception was the King. He stood in the center of his yard with head erect, an alert tenseness in every muscle, poising as lightly on his feet as a runner waiting the starting signal, every nerve and fiber atingle, and yet gloriously unafraid.

It was thus that Satan saw him, and the stout fence quivered with the fierceness of the impact as he hurled himself against it, while the air reverberated with his unearthly clamor. Surprised and chagrined that the weaker creature did not flee before his vituperative threats he thrust his coarse muzzle as far as it would go through the woven meshes of the fence and emitted a series of snarls that had often proved effective.

McElwood, searching frantically for a fence stake or some other weapon equally familiar to the hands of an angry Irishman, paused abruptly as he caught sight of the King.

Slowly, calmly, with never a hint of threat or displeasure in his manner, he was advancing regally toward the raging dog. Instantly the snarling became more vehement but now even the man could detect the uneasy note in it and his wild, Irish heart jumped ecstatically.

"It's your number he's got, ye domned yeller cur," he cried. "Ye've called him all the fightin' words in your dictionary and now that he's comin' over to ask ye what ye mean by it, ye're scared. Look at the tail of ye! Bechune your legs, already. Ye'd like to run but ye dassn't."

McElwood was right. Satan was worried but he had gone too far to withdraw and he still had a measure of confidence in the efficacy of that fierce growl to avert disaster. Too late he discovered his mistake. The King's head was within a foot of that ugly muzzle, and still advancing, when the dog suddenly decided it was time to retreat. And in that instant the King struck.

With a deadly accuracy and speed that nothing but a rattlesnake could have equaled, his head flashed forward and his needlelike teeth closed over the nose and lips of the brute before him. Satan had already started his backward leap and, as those white teeth drove their length in his tortured nose he gave that leap new impetus. The effect was all that the Irishman or the fox could have desired. The momentum of that backward surge drew the King's slim muzzle through the mesh of the fence half the length of his powerful jaws. His fangs were still deeply imbedded in his adversary's nose, and now the restraining wires, pressing firmly about his upper and lower jaws, prevented his opening them even had he been so inclined.

The dog, in a perfect frenzy of fear and pain, redoubled his efforts to escape. Something had to give way. The wire fence would have held an angry bull; the teeth of the fox were only a little less powerful than tempered steel and so it was the tissues of nose and lips that parted.

Satan fled precipitately, clamoring his woes vociferously to an unfeeling world. The Irishman jeered at him openly as he ran promiscuously about, seeking some cover where he might hide from those countless pairs of eyes that were now watching him from every hut entrance.

"Maybe now that'll be teachin' ye to keep your nose out of other folks' business," McElwood called after him. "It's close ye come to losin' it altogether and divil a bit would I cared if ye had. Ye'll not try that trick again, I'm thinkin'!"

In this, too, he was right. Satan's nose never again, by any chance, came within a foot of the wires and an even greater distance than that marked what he considered the safety zone when he passed the King's inclosure. Always when he saw that regal animal his eyes widened and glowed with a baleful light. In his cowardly heart he knew he would never dare wage a battle against that adversary when the odds were not decidedly in his favor, but if opportunity ever offered, when he could catch this particular fox at a disadvantage, he would know in full measure the sweetness of revenge.

And, despite the fact that each runway was inclosed with a woven-wire fence nine feet in height and the entire colony surrounded by another fence of the same material, the time came when the King stood outside, as free as the glorious north wind he so eagerly sniffed. That time came, and, later, came the opportunity of which Satan had often dreamed in his hours of restless slumber.

It happened on a night in late September. One of those terrific thunderstorms, that are so characteristic of northern Maine in the early fall, swept over the valley. Driving low over the western mountains it came in cyclonic fury. The rain was torrential. Crash after reverberating crash shook the earth while the echoes beat back and forth deafeningly between the towering hills.

Nearly all the other foxes crept tremblingly into their huts, but the King sprang lightly to the top of his and stood there, statuelike, watching the storm. His was an outer yard and but a scant four feet separated it from the outer fence. Between the two fences at this point a lone pine tree stood, its mighty, storm-tossed branches beating rhythmic time to the wild, staccato music of the tempest.

Standing alone on the little man-made hut, in the wild fury of the gale, the King knew a calm, satisfying content. The hammering blast of the wind, the sting of the rain, driven slantwise with bulletlike velocity, the creaking of the tortured branches and, dominating all else, the blinding, incessant flare of the lightning with its nerve shattering accompaniment of thunder filled him with wild exultation.

This was nature as he knew it; as he had known it for countless ages past. Nature in an exuberant, boisterous mood it is true, but a kind, loving mother notwithstanding. And the King, despite the encompassing strands of steel, despite the seven generations of captive forbears, was still Nature's child.

Suddenly, as he stood gazing upward, there came a swift bluish flash—a blinding redness as if the world were wrapped in seething flame—a rending crash above him as of wood riven asunder and then, in that instant, quietness and darkness: the quietness and darkness of eternal night.

It was the cool north wind that revived him, and for a long time he lay panting, drinking in the sweet oxygen in deep, thankful inhalations. He was aware of a peculiar numbness in his muscles, an extreme lassitude so out of keeping with his usual vital energy that he struggled to his feet in alarm and looked about him. The storm had passed. It still rumbled faintly in the east but overhead the stars were shining. In the west the low hanging moon sailed in silvery splendor over the treetops.

Gazing at it, the King was dimly aware of a change in its appearance. Always before, unless nearly overhead its face had been crisscrossed by heavy wires—the wires that barred him from freedom. Now it was unmarred. Its soft white rays fell calmly on the surface of the yard and left no zigzag pattern of prison bars.

Then the King saw what had hitherto been unnoticed; cleft cleanly from the trunk by the lightning bolt, one of the giant branches of the old tree had fallen across the wires beneath, crushing them to earth. To the King, only, Nature had bestowed this boon that was more to him than life itself. He stepped daintily up on the fallen limb, traversed a part of its length until he was outside the inclosure, sprang softly off on the dripping grass, free, as Nature had intended all her children should be.

For a time he stood there, scenting the air for a trace of his one known enemy, but Satan had noisily begged for admission at McElwood's door at the first heavy crash of thunder and was still hidden beneath the calmly sleeping Irishman's bed, tremblingly aware of the faint, grumbling mutter of the departing storm.

As silently as a shadow the King crossed the long meadow that lay between him and the heavy wood instinct prompted him to seek. Halfway across, a fat meadow mouse, foraging for beetles, fled, squeaking in fright. Without conscious thought the King sprang sidewise and snapped up the fleeing rodent. He was not especially hungry but the morsel of warm flesh awoke vague, dormant memories and gave him a pleasantly contented feeling.

Reaching the timber at last his attention was instantly arrested by a faint nibbling sound and an odor that was strangely familiar. McElwood raised Belgian hares as a hobby as well as for the considerable profit it yielded, and when the wind was in the right quarter, the King had often had their scent wafted to his nostrils.

This particular odor had an added hint of the wild in it but the fox placed it instantly as something highly edible and he turned toward the sound. A few feet away he espied the quarry. The tremendous wind had broken the top from a thrifty young poplar and hurled it to the ground. A fat, old, snowshoe rabbit had found it and now sat nibbling contentedly at the tender tips.

Stealing a step nearer the King catapulted forward. There was a frightened squeak, a lightning snap of those slim jaws and again silence. But, as the King stood over the limp body, he knew a perfect happiness. For him life had no terrors. He was free, the master of his own destiny. Food there was in plenty for those with the skill to acquire it and he had proved his ability.

He ate the rabbit leisurely, then hunted out a decaying stump. Springing upon this he sniffed the wind for a moment, turned about several times and then curled up in a compact, furry ball. In another minute he was asleep.

When McElwood found the broken fence, in the early

morning, he made haste to telephone the directors. That they were annoyed by the loss was evident. They arrived, some three hours later, in a big, high-powered machine and brought with them a man truly remarkable by the contrast between himself and these sleek, well-groomed men of affairs.

He was a little, shriveled old man with the most remarkable set of white whiskers McElwood had ever seen. They seemed to defy the law of gravity, standing straight out from his face, hiding every feature but the very tip of a particularly red nose and two little deep-set eyes that darted furtively here and there and saw everything while apparently seeing nothing. His clothes were overalls and frock that once had been blue but were now the dull, lifeless gray of weathered oak. Under his arm he carried a burlap bag, and the contents, although not bulky, appeared heavy. When he moved about they gave forth a clanking sound.

"Mr. Sims, Mr. McElwood." The fat director did the honors. "Mr. Sims is rather a celebrity where fox trappers congregate. The best in New England, you know. We have arranged with him to catch the Sable King for us."

McElwood laughed. "It's an airplane you'll be needin', Mr. Sims, I'm thinkin'. Them pipestem legs of yourn ain't equal to it. He's farther away now than you could walk in a week—and still goin'."

"You're a liar," said Mr. Sims, so matter-of-factly that McElwood, hot-headed Irishman that he was, believed it implicitly. "That fox ain't two miles from here and won't be for a month. He's got to get used to bein' free; learn to take care of himself before he leaves the country. He'll come back to the yards more than once, most likely. He'll be lonesome for a while. I'll have him in less than a week."

"Do that," said the fat director, "and we'll add another fifty to the hundred we promised you. It will be cheap at that. We value that fox at five thousand dollars."

"I'll get him," Mr. Sims informed them, "but it'll take about a week. I want to make sure of him. Get him takin' my bait reg'lar and then I'll nail him. Don't want to make a slip-up on it. Just pinch his toes a little and he'd light out of here as if the devil was after him. Well, I'll look round a bit."

Forthwith Mr. Sims deposited the burlap bag on McElwood's steps and then divested himself of his faded frock, thereby exposing to view an undershirt that would have put to shame a tropical sunset for vividness of color. He went directly to the yards and surveyed the broken fence for a moment, noted the position of the fallen limb and other, seemingly unimportant, details. Then, turning, he surveyed the distant landscape.

"Um-hm," he said. "Followed that swale to the

meadow, of course; easiest walking. Then across the meadow in a straight line; that's the way they travel. Hit the woods about there, I reckon. I'll look it over a bit."

Mr. Sims entered the wood within thirty feet of the spot where the King had killed the rabbit. His diligent eyes noted the little bundles of torn fur instantly and he crossed over to them. He regarded them idly for a minute, stirring one with a toe, then poked it tentatively with a clawlike finger. "Um-hm." Then, so silently that he might have been a thistledown, he drifted cautiously down wind.

A hundred yards he floated, then turned obliquely deeper into the woods. Again he turned and now, like a shadow, he glided back into the wind, his little eyes seeing everything in photographic detail.

A moment later he stopped. The midday sun, riding high and clear in the heavens, struck full on a large, weathered stump a hundred feet ahead. The stump was crowned with a furry ball; a glistening ball that reflected the light with all the sheen and luster of the fur seal. Mr. Sims watched it intently for a long time. Then he breathed a long sigh; a sigh of satisfaction. "Um-hm," he whispered. "Um-hm."

Two hours later the King awoke. There was a faint, pleasurable odor in his nostrils, suggestive of some hitherto unknown delicacy. He uncoiled himself deliberately and rose to his feet, stretching as he did so, much as a cat does when rising from its bed. The King was not especially hungry but, as he sniffed the freighted air, he felt a little anticipatory thrill.

Straight to a little juniper bush he followed the scent and located it immediately as coming from a newly excavated hole beneath a sheltering branch. Then, instinctively, he paused, tensely alert. His nose told him that here was some inanimate thing that was distinctly edible, a dainty tidbit that required no delicate stalking and lightninglike spring to capture. It was his for the taking, and yet—elusive, almost imperceptible, there was the slightest taint of man smell in the air. He could distinguish it as a separate entity from the more engrossing odors into which it had miraculously merged—but it was there.

Another hour of clear sunshine and it would have vanished forever, and the story of the Sable King would have been not worth the telling.

Hitherto, with the exception of the last few hours, since he had been weaned, he had known no food other than that prepared by the hand of man. It had been served to him in dishes handled repeatedly by human beings. The taint of their bodies and breath had polluted the very air he breathed, yet he had eaten the things they placed before him, eagerly and without fear.

Now, in less than twenty-four hours since he had become free, he found himself rigidly alert, instinctively hesitating to accept a tempting delicacy to which clung the almost imperceptible odor of man. Man! The only species of the animal kingdom that might, by the wildest stretch of imagination, be called a friend.

It was the wraiths of a thousand ancestors, long since returned to the dust, crying to him to shun this scent that meant death. And, strange as it may seem, the King heard.

He side-stepped gingerly and approached the bush from another quarter. Pausing on a little knoll he peered sharply at the small mound of new earth from whence came that engrossing smell. Strips of salted fish, roasted over an open fire and rolled in comb honey, to which a few drops of oil of anise had been added, was the lure that enticed him. The saliva dripped from his bright red tongue as a flaw in the wind brought the delectable odor home more strongly to his nostrils.

The King advanced, cautiously, scanning every bit of ground before he ventured to set his dainty foot upon it and, at last, came within reaching distance of the prize. Delicately he raked one of the tempting morsels toward him and ate it with avidity. Another and another followed and nothing happened, excepting that his appetite was increased rather than satiated.

He stepped out boldly now and devoured the delicacies as he found them, even pawing the dirt away from one piece which his sensitive nose told him was buried in the freshly turned earth.

When the last fragment had been devoured he hunted assiduously in that vicinity for more but, failing to locate any, departed, with the coming of night, to the meadow. Here he stalked mice, with fair success, until the eastern sky grew pink. Back in the woods again he found another stump and was soon asleep.

He awoke at dusk, and memory surged, instantly, within him. Again he went to the juniper bush. Like the widow's cruse, the supply was again replenished, and again the faint, man odor was discernible, but the King paused but momentarily. The spicy tang of the savory fare was in his nostrils and he advanced boldly. Again he ate it all and nosed among the leaves for a few scattered crumbs.

The next night and the night immediately following, he gathered his bounty from the laps of the gods. On the morning of the next day it rained, a steady, cold downpour that drove him from his unprotected stump to the shelter of a crevice in the rocks far up on the hillside.

In the early evening the rain ceased; a light westerly wind lifted and scattered the clouds, and bright stars twinkled in the rifts thus formed. As the first one peeped forth the King emerged from his lair and paused to sniff the clean, fresh air.

Instantly his ears snapped forward, the heavy brush of his tail lifted and increased in size perceptibly. He stepped forward eagerly. There was a mincing, springy lift to his forefeet, an electric quality in his bearing that enhanced his natural beauty a hundredfold.

He was not only a King but a lover for, borne on to him by the wind, mingled with the spicy aroma of the fallen leaves and the freshly scattered pine needles, came the age-old vision of a fairy footed vixen dancing enticingly before him over snow covered, moonlit barrens: dancing ever more alluringly, and drawing him ever on and on.

Thus, boldly, unquestioningly, the King followed the Lorelei to the juniper. The scent was stronger here and with it was mingled the odor of honey. He paused a moment, sniffing, and then advanced. A slender twig, hitherto unnoticed, was looped across his path. Unhesitatingly he lifted a delicate forefoot and stepped over it.

There was a sharp snap, a shrill tinkle of moving chain, a wild futile leap to elude the trap: another and another, each more frenzied than the one preceding it, until the flying grapple hooked securely on the springy branch of a stunted hemlock, and progress suddenly ceased.

The Sable King was no longer free. A Number 2,

double-jawed trap gripped his right forefoot well above the toes, and no power within himself could shake off that thing of steel that instinct told him meant death. Poor King! How many of your kind have felt that sudden sting. How many, many thousands, have waited, like you, through the interminable hours of a never-ending night; waited for the coming of dawn—of man—and of death!

In the early half light of another morning the fat director was awakened by the insistent ringing of his telephone and, in answering it, heard McElwood's voice on the wire.

"It's a doctor we're needin' up here this fine mornin'," that cheerful Celt informed him. "That professional trapper of yours caught one damn' fine cold yesterday, paddlin' around in the rain all day, and its pneumonia he's got this mornin' or I'm a fool. He's that hot I could fry me bacon and eggs on him and save washin' me skillet if I had the time to do it. He's crazy as a bedbug, hollerin' for some one to help him bring in his fox and frettin' for fear ye won't pay him the hundred and fifty ye promised him. He'll be needin' that same to pay his funeral expenses if ye don't be after gettin' here quick with a doctor."

The director's question informed the listening operator just how that party felt regarding capital and labor.

"Has he got the fox?" he asked.

"Sure, he says he has. He's ravin' about never missin'

one in twenty years. A divil of a mess it is if you're askin' me, what with him flat on his back for a couple of weeks, most likely, the King with his foot in a trap somewheres and me not knowin' whether he's in this county or the next. It's reinforcements I'm needin'."

"I'll be there in two hours if I can pry a doctor out of bed at this time in the morning. We will find the King easily enough; let Satan hunt him up. Be ready when I get there."

McElwood fed his foxes, swearing methodically the while. "Sure, it's several kinds of a domned fool you were, King, to stick around here when the whole world was before ye. For why didn't ye get out of here? Serves ye right, if it's caught ye are, for not havin' brains enough to beat it. Now you'll be losin' yer liberty, and a foot, too, most likely."

Back again, in the cottage, he swore as steadily and with even more fervor at the delirious trapper. Swore, even as he applied the hot fomentations to the laboring chest and cold compresses to the fevered brow.

"Domned if I know why it's pourin' more water on you, I am, and you that soaked only yesterday that you looked for all the world like a kitten that had fell in the rain barrel. Still, I suppose if I let you dry out, and a sudden breeze should spring up, you'd blow out through the window as easy as a leaf out of the dictionary. Sure, you're that thin that I'd set your weight somewhere between six and seven pounds lighter than a straw hat. How you could catch a cold of that size, and bring it home, is more than I can understand. I wonder, now, how would a good, stiff, shot o' whisky suit ye? Sure, I'd give it to ye in a minute if I dared to—and had it."

Thus he attended the sick man, pausing momentarily to snatch a bite of cold breakfast and to carefully wipe the oil from the rifling of a .303 Savage, his one prized possession and a weapon that was inconceivably accurate in his steady hands.

"You're wonderin', I suppose, what I'm takin' a rifle for to bring in a trapped fox," he told the tossing trapper. "For your information I'll tell ye that it's open season on deer now. I never get what I'm huntin' for, so maybe if I start out lookin' for a deer I'll find your domned fox. The old darlint shoots a bit high the first shot, with the oil in her, which you know as well as me if you know anything, which you don't this mornin'. Where's that hellhound? Come out from behind that stove, ye black faced son of the Old Boy himself, and eat this breakfast that ye don't deserve."

When the fat director arrived with the doctor McElwood's cottage was in order and the hot cloths had not once grown cold on the patient's chest or the cold ones warm on his brow. The medico nodded approval as he shook his thermometer. "You have adopted the proper method," he told the Irishman. "I would say, offhand, that we will pull him through very nicely. Now, go get your fox. That seems to be the all important thing just now with the three of you."

Twenty minutes later, Satan, making a long cast well ahead of the puffing director and the silent McElwood, suddenly paused and swung about to face a low juniper a few yards to his left. For a moment he hesitated, the hair rising stiffly on his back, then, with a villainous bellow, he plunged toward it.

McElwood saw him as he jumped, and snapped out an order to his employer. "There's your fox, I'm thinkin'. Get a move on ye now, or there won't be enough of his hide left to make a flyin' jib to a wheelbarrow." The last words were flung over his shoulder, for already he was running in long, springy strides toward that distant point where he felt a tragedy was about to happen.

But, to the King, the tragedy had already occurred. When the double jawed trap had snapped about his delicate forefoot the instinct implanted in him from a thousand progenitors had whispered that this thing was death. His first frantic plunges had told him there was no escape.

[27]

The upper jaws had bedded themselves in the soft pad of his paw, the lower ones fitted gently over the toes and prevented any possible chance of gnawing off these members when they had become sufficiently numb to render the amputation painless.

The King was a captive. That he knew, and no power within himself could remove this thing that spelled an end to his existence.

Through the long hours of the night he waited, inactive, denied either movement or the luxury of curling into the warm ball that retained the bodily heat, and when at last the sun crept over the horizon he was stiff and cramped in every muscle, weakened by the night's interminable hours and the unaccustomed fast, yet when he heard that malevolent roar from his old enemy he was instantly alert and whirled, like a flash of light, to face the oncoming charge.

It was thus that Satan found him as he surged in that mad rush through the tangled juniper brush. In that moment the King was majestic. Facing death, fettered by the trap, cold, cramped and weakened by exhaustion, he faced his sworn enemy in what he knew to be his last battle, with a cool, calculating calmness that was superb.

In the instant that Satan saw him thus he hesitated and again the old thrill of fear flashed over him. Then, by some

unexplainable sense, he knew that the King was at a disadvantage and, with another roar, he hurled himself forward for that revenge he had waited so long to attain.

Nothing but the very fierceness of that charge saved
the fox from instant death. The grapple, attached by a short
chain to the trap, had anchored itself firmly in the hemlock and there was but a scant yard of chain. When, at the
end of his mighty leap, the wolfish jaws of the dog
crunched down on the bone and tissue of the fox, the heavy
impact of that swift moving body accomplished that which
the King's weight alone could not do; the paw slipped,
unharmed, from the clinging jaws.

Instantly Satan regretted his hasty attack, for those
needlelike fangs were everywhere about his body, cutting
to the limit of their length at every lightning stroke; but
his own jaws were clamped, crushingly, over the back and
short ribs of the fox, and he knew if he could but maintain
that hold for a minute the victory would be his.

He was not alone in this knowledge. The King became
suddenly aware of that deadly, numbing pain and, doub-
ling back on himself, buried his teeth in the nose that,
although healed, was still very, very tender.

A thoroughbred would have borne it for another moment while he crunched the harder, but Satan was a cur
and he whimpered with the agony of it. Then, at a twisting

wrench at that tortured member, he opened his jaws and howled even as he had howled that other morning when the King had punished him thus.

When those jaws relaxed the King gave another vicious twist and leaped free. He had no desire to continue the battle. His hind quarters were as leaden weights and only sluggishly obeyed the brain that willed them to move. One forepaw was badly swollen and ached excruciatingly now that the blood once more circulated through it. He was exhausted and well-nigh done to death, yet he faced the big dog fearlessly, ready to resume the battle if that vicious brute advanced an inch.

At that moment there came to his ear the crashing of brush under the feet of hurrying men and a quick glance showed him McElwood running toward him and, some distance behind, another larger and badly winded runner.

Man! Man the killer! All the old primal instinct flashed back upon him. Man! Death! The Sable King turned with what speed his spent muscles would lend him and fled.

Had they been alone Satan would never have risked another encounter but the proximity of man gave him courage and he dashed toward the slow moving fox. When his huge jaws closed on the quarry the end would come quickly and he rapidly cut down the intervening distance.

It was then that the fat director looked up. What he

saw was his famous fox, free, running away from a dog that frothed and drooled in his eagerness to be in at the death and, as that glorious fox made his last, gallant effort for life, all the director saw was so many dollars slipping from his grasp. Gone were the chances of raising a new and valuable strain: gone also the thousand or more dollars the pelt would bring. All gone!

But no! Not quite. There was one chance left. "Don't let him get away," he gasped and the Irishman heard. "The rifle, man. Shoot."

McElwood stopped, square footed, and the rifle leaped to his shoulder in the graceful flash of the accomplished snap shooter. The flat crash of dense nitro snapped on the frosty air and, fifty yards away, Satan somersaulted cleanly as 165 grains of lead tore through his heart.

"Nice work," McElwood whispered as he turned to face the director, then, lifting his voice he shouted. "It's a bum shot I am, this mornin', what with the runnin' and all. Sure, it's the dog that I killed. Now what do ye know about that?"

The fat man stopped and wiped his perspiring brow. "I don't know anything about it," he shouted back, "but there's no law in the United States to prevent a man from thinking what he damn pleases."

Out of sight among the trees the Sable King paused

and listened. There was no sound of pursuit. As he stood there he could feel the blood pulsing strongly back into those numbed legs as his heart pounded energetically from his exertions. Then a breath of wind fanned him. He turned and sniffed it eagerly. It was the cool north wind.

KING OF PARADISE VALLEY

THE Sable King was tired—very tired—yet he ran steadily on and, as unerringly as the needle of a compass, his nose pointed ever northward. The Northland, that vast area of frozen barrens and moonlit wastes was the land of his forefathers and, by the kind act of a merciful providence, his inheritance.

Despite the fatigue of his body the mind of the magnificent black fox knew a great content. Seven generations of his ancestors had been raised in captivity and he, until a short week before, had known no freedom other than that afforded by the close confines of his prison yard.

Now a thousand generations of ancestors, long since returned to the dust whence they came, were calling him to the land of their nativity and the King, man-reared though he was, heard and was answering the call.

That one short week of freedom had been fraught with peril but now he was free—free. Behind him—many weary miles behind—lay the Maine State Fox Farms, the last outpost of civilization south of the great woods.

Ahead, through many weary miles of virgin forest and mossy glen, of perpendicular mountainsides and peaceful valleys, lay the Northland. Something within the King, yet something outside his consciousness, demanded of

those weary leg muscles that they continue to function—
and the weary muscles obeyed.

In two weeks he had covered a thousand miles and was
so thin that McElwood would not have recognized him,
but his muscles were hardening daily and he traveled with
greater ease than at first. In a month he had more than
doubled the distance and was gaining flesh, for he had
learned now to take time to stalk his prey rather than to
depend on the headlong rush he had hitherto employed.
He had learned that, in the end, it required less time and
was far more productive of results.

The big, snowshoe hares were everywhere abundant,
but theirs was the caution of the much-hunted weakling,
and the rustle of a twig would send them bounding away.
However, the King readily learned the manner of the
soundless approach, creeping, belly to earth, within striking distance and, when he made his final spring, few indeed
were the lesser creatures that eluded his meteoric assault.

Thus he ate and rested his glorious body and then resumed his pilgrimage. Neither rushing torrents nor broad,
slow moving rivers deterred him: neither ice nor snow nor
wintry winds turned him aside, for the Northland—the
land of his forefathers—was calling, and his inner consciousness heard—and obeyed.

For three months the King traveled, as straight as a

homing pigeon, toward the land of his desire. At last there came a day when he stood on the jagged summit of a low-lying mountain and surveyed the world below. To the north stretched the vast, level white expanse of the frozen Arctic Ocean. East and west the mountain range sloped gradually down to the sea level, making a basin that embraced more than a hundred square miles.

Looking down upon it, the Sable King suddenly knew a great content. He had reached the promised land. Instinct told him that that vast amphitheater would be a veritable Mecca for one of his breed. Bird life would be abundant in the summer and the stunted willows would afford unlimited food for the countless hordes of snowshoe hares that crouched low in the sheltering cover.

Long and steadfastly he gazed at the scene below, then, as a monarch descends from his jeweled throne, he walked majestically forward. All signs of haste had departed; there was a regal grace in every movement of his beautiful body as, with head held high, his forefeet lifting with springy suppleness, he advanced as a king should advance when entering his own domain.

For two months he lived in utter content. He explored every nook and cranny of his kingdom and found it good. He saw many other foxes but none of his strain. Little, blue arctic foxes and foxes of pure white were intermingled with the more common reds but, for a time, he failed to see a single individual of his own color.

Then, one night, when the northern lights were gleaming, lighting the heavens with their weird glare, he encountered a battle scarred old veteran, identical in color to those relatives he had left in the fox farm pens.

The King was inclined to be friendly but the stranger met his overtures with a warning snarl that was so venomous that he halted abruptly, whereupon the stranger turned and resumed his journey, his pointed nose sniffing eagerly at a row of dainty footprints in the newly fallen snow.

The King waited a decent interval, for the rules of etiquette are strictly observed in the wilds, then advanced and, in turn, sniffed at the dainty footprints. That they were of another of his kind he knew, but there was something vaguely disquieting about them. He had a slight inclination to follow but recollection of that grim old campaigner deterred him. As yet he had never gone in pursuit of trouble, and only a vague hint of curiosity urged him on so, after a few moments, he resumed his interrupted way.

However the next night found him on the same route and, when he neared the open space where he had met the surly old warrior the previous night, he waited. He had, with that unexplainable ability of the wild creature, timed his arrival almost to the minute. He had hardly paused ere there came to his ears, a clear, little, excited and exciting bark from the thick fringe of willows that skirted the glade, and out into the moonlit opening danced such a fox as but few humans have ever seen. In color she was the exact duplicate of the Sable King. Each hair was tipped with a mere pinpoint of gleaming silver while the undercoat was a perfect black, with all the velvety softness of the sable and all the sheen and luster of the fur seal.

There, under that arctic sky, she danced. Danced is the only word which adequately describes it. A wild, barbaric symphony of motion, her slim body twisting in rapid, sinuous convolutions, then suddenly stiffening into beautiful, statuesque poses. Fascinated, scarcely breathing, the King watched as the slim vixen danced on and on. Above, the northern lights crackled and flared and the little glade magically became a great stage that no master craftsman could ever hope to equal, as no master playwright could hope to write the swift moving drama that followed.

It began abruptly. The fairy-footed creature had, in her mad gyrations, danced well out into the center of the glade when a flaw in the wind wafted her scent to the nostrils of the Sable King, and, in that instant, he knew that this was the goal of his desires. That old, primordial, half formed dream had reached its conclusion, and Eve, delectable as of old, was dancing in the garden.

[37]

The King advanced.

Instantly, from the willows, came a warning snarl and the scarred old legioner stalked out menacingly, into the open. Not by the most minute fraction of time did the King hesitate. In his carriage there was a new regalness, a new steadfastness of purpose, a certain, eager longing for the impending fray and a consciousness of the age old adage anent the victor and the spoils of war.

The vixen had ceased her pirouetting at the first challenge and now sat on her haunches, her lolling tongue a vivid carmine in the moonlight as she gazed, with quickened interest, at the advancing rivals.

They met with a clash. The old fox had a score of these amorous duels to his credit and had learned the value of a sudden assault on the morale of the enemy, but there was youth and fire in the heart of the King and the manner of approach was to his liking. At one moment they were apart, two separate entities; the next moment they were as one, a seething, galvanic mass of writhing, distorted muscle and gleaming fangs—needlelike fangs which gleamed white for a moment in the moonlight ere they, too, assumed a carmine hue.

Flesh and blood could not long endure the cataclysmic fury of that deadly strife. It continued for perhaps a minute and then came a gurgling rattle as sharp teeth slashed deeply through a jugular vein; a succession of floundering attempts to rise that rapidly grew weaker; a disentangling of that welded mass as one supple body stepped warily away from that other limp form on the snow. For him the play had ended and the curtain had dropped on the final act.

For the Sable King, however, a new act had begun for, across the glittering snows, a slim form advanced to meet him. He greeted her with extended nose and a friendly sniff, then dropping to the snow, fell to licking his many wounds. She hovered over him for a moment and the King experienced a new and wholly delightful sensation. There was an ugly slash high up on his shoulder that he could not reach. It was paining excruciatingly when suddenly the pain ceased. A carmine tongue, other than his own, was applying an efficacious first aid.

It was spring. Not spring as we of the Southlands know it but rather a less rigorous winter. Rivulets seeped out of the snow covered hillsides and, joining other rivulets, became miniature brooks, dashing madly downward in their irresistible rush toward the sea. Jagged rocks lifted their brown sides higher, daily, from the enveloping snows and the skies were a tranquil blue overhead.

It was weather that should have brought contentment but the King was distinctly uneasy. A new actor had made his entrance on the stage; an actor whose appearance threatened to turn that delightful little domestic drama, in which the King and his mate were playing the leading roles, into a grim tragedy at any moment. That new actor was *man*.

Big Pierre Laroux had run his trap line farther north than usual that winter and with unusual success. Few men in the Northland excelled him in the ability to bring in a good catch of fur but this year Fortune had been especially kind and his pile of pelts exceeded, by far, any of his previous records.

For years he had heard of the fabled Paradise Valley where even golden martin were plentiful but, as yet, he had never seen that enchanted valley. Realizing that he had now taken the maximum amount of fur from his line, and still leave enough to assure a plentiful supply the following winter, he yielded to a sudden impulse, packed a few supplies and a dozen traps on his skeleton sled, cached his furs securely, strapped on his snowshoes and started, forthwith.

A week before, he had paused, as had the Sable King, on the brink of that overhanging cliff and looked down on the peaceful valley below. He was all French and now, as he gazed down on that beautiful valley, his Frenchman's heart was strangely stirred.

"Mon Dieu," he breathed, "She's been long tam I've travel' thees co'ntry and ain't never saw noddin' dat's begin for compare wit' dat. She's one new co'ntries for Pierre Laroux an' she's satisfy to me. Fur? W'y, fur ron all hover dat place. I'm go down for see it some more."

Pierre was well down to the level when he stopped suddenly and crouched low. Slowly—very slowly—he exhaled his breath in a long drawn, incredulous sigh of wonder and unbelief. The sigh was permissible. Under the circumstances anything, or nothing, would have been equally so for, at that moment, Pierre Laroux, uneducated, uncouth son of the Northland, was gazing on that which no other mortal had ever yet beheld.

Around a tangle of stunted shrubbery a score of yards away stepped a pair of foxes that might only be pictured in a particularly vivid dream. Black they were; as black as the Stygian blackness of the darkest night and yet not wholly black, but burnished platinum where the sun struck those glistening pinpoints of white. In the slanting rays of the brilliant sun their coats glimmered and shone and refracted the light rays as a perfect diamond does under a powerful arc light.

Unwinkingly the big Frenchman watched them until the brush had swallowed them up; then he bared his head, almost reverently, as he gazed at the spot where they had disappeared.

"Mon Dieu," he whispered, "I don't know for sure

whedder I see dat or no but I'm go'n stay on dis co'ntry 'till I catch dem two feller if I stay t'ree mont'."

It was a day later that the King learned of the new presence, and it happened in this manner. With his mate he was slowly moving down the valley on what, to him, seemed a foolish, fruitless quest. There was warmth in the sun and he, had he been allowed to choose, would have selected one of those bare rocks, in some nook where the wind did not penetrate, and slept in comfort for the duration of that sunlight, but the slim little mate willed otherwise.

For days now a great uneasiness had possessed her. She traveled incessantly, exploring nooks and crevices in the ledges, and even dug experimentally on a little knoll where the snow had melted but, after smearing her face and legs with the sticky mud, she desisted and again resumed her aimless wandering. The King followed dutifully where she led but showed little interest, other than a vague discontent, in the proceedings.

On this particular day he had stood back while she laboriously climbed a rocky slope, from which the snows had largely melted, and thrust an inquisitive nose into the rectangular opening beneath a jutting stone. Suddenly she turned and sniffed the air as she did at the scent of close lying game. The King was instantly alert and in a moment was at her side.

He caught it at once—a faint, far reaching, spicy odor, suggestive of something distinctly edible but there was a certain something—a faint suspicion of another smell.

His mate had swung, quartering, into the wind, running the scent down to its source much as a good setter locates a wily ruffed grouse. The King followed close and, within him memory, reason, instinct (call it what you will) stirred. There came a flaw in the wind and the scent vanished; it veered again, bringing back with it that peculiar taint the King's delicate nose had detected and, in that moment, the fox *knew*.

Man! Man, the killer. With one lunging leap he overtook his mate, snarled horribly at her and even drove his white teeth admonishingly into her slim shoulder. Bewildered, she would have evaded him and pressed on but he thrust her back bodily and nipped her flank.

When at last she understood that this unknown scent was a thing to be shunned as is death itself, the King leaped away from her, running straightaway for a hundred yards in an apparent frenzy of fear. Laboriously she followed as best she could and, when she reached the spot where he was waiting, she was panting heavily. He licked her shoulder while she rested and when she again started on her aimless quest the King was at her side.

The next morning Pierre read the story in the telltale

tracks in the snow and he was enough of a sportsman to take his defeat philosophically. "Dat time you beat me, Meestair Fox," he chuckled, "but we try some more. Dat ol' dog fox, she's have his toe peench sometam an' she's know wot trap is, for sure. But Pierre know two, t'ree t'ing his self. He catch a trap on dose fox's foot hinside one week, I'll bet t'ousand dollar."

But Big Pierre did not win that bet. Every artifice known to the trappers of the far north he tried but to no avail. There is truth in that old adage that "curiosity killed the cat." Curiosity has killed millions of four-footed creatures other than those of the cat family. Suspicion may be strong that things are not exactly as they seem but the desire to learn *why* lures them on, and when at last they have learned, it is, alas, too late.

In the mind of the King, however, there was no curiosity concerning man. The emotion had been sated long since and now, when that odor came to his nostrils, he paused only to locate it and then proceeded at once, driving his mate before him, in an opposite direction.

At last there came a day when Big Pierre was forced to admit that he was beaten. "Dose fox, she's smarter feller dan Pierre," he grumbled. "One tam I t'ink she's go home on my pack an' I be please for show dose skin to ever'body on de pos'. One tam I t'ink dat but not some more. Dat ol' fox, she's laugh hup his sleeve an' say, 'Pierre, you one hell smart trapper. You good feller for set snare for rabbit, an' you catch lynx dat dam' fool for catch his self, but ol' fox, she's smarter dan two Frenchman. Go home and whittle de bateau for dose kid. You hall right for dat.' "

So Pierre took up his last, careful set, lashed his pack securely and swung it across his broad shoulders. Without hesitation he had obeyed the whimsical fancy that had lured him to this spot and, as instantly, he obeyed that fancy which called him from it.

On the ragged summit he paused and turned for one last look at Paradise Valley. The slanting sun touched the budding willows with a golden glow; brooks purled and babbled in rich, silver cascades, downward toward the sea. The brown earth steamed on the sheltered hillsides where in a few days the anemone would bloom. A quarter mile below, a placid pool, spring fed, emptied its contents into a brook that wound its crooked way tumultuously downward. Even as he looked he saw the pool's amethyst surface suddenly break and shimmer in widening ripples where a giant trout had jumped for the first fly of the season. On the sandy bank above the pool an otter paused—or was it an otter?

Pierre leaned forward, his keen eyes peering sharply downward. For a long minute he gazed, then slowly lowered his pack to the ground. Methodically and unhurriedly he undid the lashings that held his rolled sleeping bag in place. The heavy woolen blankets that lined it he removed, and stood up with the waterproofed canvas bag in his hands.

"Now, Meestair Fox," he said, "we see if you mak' fon of Frenchman some more. Dis tam I t'ink Pierre go'n' laugh his self." With the canvas bag in his hands he started down the mountainside.

At last the King's mate had found a spot to her liking. The sandy bank above the quiet pool had thawed quickly and could be easily excavated, while its close proximity to the spring would prevent its drying to an extent where a cave-in would be likely to occur.

She had looked the situation over carefully from every angle and had, at last, selected a spot near the top of the bank where she now began digging furiously.

The Sable King immediately showed interest in her busy activity, suspecting she was trying to unearth a burrowing rodent, but his keen nostrils could detect no scent of game. Nevertheless he hovered close as she worked, for there was a new, subtle quality of eagerness in her every movement, a plaintive note in her faint whimperings when she encountered some obstacle that, for a few moments, rendered her activity ineffectual. He watched her intently and when, at last, she had burrowed more than her length in that level strata of sand he, too, whined eagerly and crept in behind her.

Here he found the earth piled high between them and, in order to be near her, he scratched it backward and heard it drop, like falling rain, into the pool below. The vixen gave him a sharp bark of approbation and thereafter he dug as diligently as she and when she paused, from sheer exhaustion, and backed, panting, toward him, he made way for her. He waited 'till she had scrambled to the level ground above and stretched out full length in the invigorating sunshine and then returned, alone, to the tunnel and fell vigorously to work. Even eight generations of forebears reared in captivity in man-made yards, yes, even whelped in man-made huts, could not kill the hereditary instinct that told him this burrow was an imperative necessity; a thing that, for the happiness and security of his mate, would brook no procrastinating methods of construction.

He did not know that spring had come far later than usual this year, nor that his mating had been early in the season. He did not know that the panting form above him would face her accouchement in a very few days and that a dry, warm chamber was absolutely necessary if their offspring were to survive in the rugged battle of life.

Instinct could not tell him this but it did tell him one

thing and that one thing was *dig*. And so the King dug and, when she had rested, the vixen came to his assistance.

So, for three days, they labored and neither darkness nor daylight swerved them from their objective. True, the King made short excursions for food while his mate lay panting just above the opening of the tunnel and, when fortune favored him with a ptarmigan or a fat rabbit he brought it to her side.

In those three days they had penetrated a depth of twelve feet. Now, under the vixen's guidance, the tunnel took a sharp upward slant. There, when she had reached the desired level, she began excavating a circular cavern three feet or more in diameter and high enough so that she might stand erect. She dug energetically but, although it was a long way to the tunnel's mouth, the King kept the passage clear. He backed out, scratching with all four feet; he came back in like manner in endless repetition and when at last she had the chamber shaped to her liking there was no loose sand on the floor of the passageway.

Now that the den was constructed, the vixen, for the first time in weeks, seemed content. She returned to the chamber and languidly began scratching her heavily furred body. That fur was loose, very loose. The spring sun and the bodily heat engendered by her strenuous labor had hastened the shedding process. As she combed deeply with her hind feet or brushed other parts with her rough tongue the hair slid from her in tufts and patches. Finding her thus engaged, the King felt an uncontrollable impulse to do likewise and, together, they covered the damp earth with a matting of warm, moisture-resisting hair.

That afternoon, from the mouth of the tunnel, the King watched a flock of geese volplane down from the heights and alight, with many loud honkings, on a marshy tract in the valley below. He was off like a dark shadow, running low and swiftly that he might be there ere some other four-footed hunter should alarm the flock. Nearing the spot he saw the old gander on an elevated mound of tufted grass, doing vigilant sentinel duty while his flock ate.

For many a year the wise old bird had faithfully performed his task, and hundreds of times his warning "honk" had cheated some marauding meat-eater of a toothsome meal, but this was destined to be his last bit of picket duty.

The King paid no attention to the gabbling flock but centered his attention on the lone guard. He spent twenty minutes in creeping the last fifteen feet, taking advantage of every tuft of grass and moving only when the gander's eyes were turned and then only by scant inches. So clever was his stalking that his leap was half completed ere the great bird was aware of danger. He had no time to move but, true to his trust, he uttered his last, warning cry to the flock even as those white teeth severed the vertebrae at the base of his skull.

With a ponderous roar of beating wings the flock surged upward and circled, in broken formation, as they waited in vain for the old leader whose massive wings beat with ever diminishing strength the earth they so long had spurned.

Not until those wings had ceased their last, faint, spasmodic twitchings did the King move. This was his first large bird but he grasped it firmly by the long neck and, although the weight was nearly equal to that of himself, swung the fat body across his back and marched firmly upward to the little home above the pool. At the entrance he barked once then, turning, backed into the hole, dragging the gander after him. A few minutes later the mattress of hair was supplemented by a downy cushion of goose feathers and the nest was complete.

Complete? Well, no. At least, not for the Sable King. The burrow, in itself, was satisfactory. In construction it was perfect but, to him, it savored too much of the *trap*. He was, by every instinct, a creature of the open, and the narrow confines of this little nest made him uneasy. There was something stifling in the thought and he stirred uneasily, then crept out into the open air.

At the mouth of the den he stood erect and eagerly

sniffed the balmy air. It was mid-afternoon and the slanting sun fell full upon the sable coat which, despite its ragged appearance, still gleamed and glistened like a raven's wing.

It was this luminous sheen that attracted the eye of Big Pierre as he paused for that backward glance down into the King's Garden of Eden. Had the King known that that eye was focused on him he might have averted the tragedy which shortly came to pass. Had he scrambled up the bank and disappeared, Pierre would have sworn goodnaturedly, and resumed his way, humbly conscious that he was no match for the animal that seemed endowed with almost superhuman cunning. Had he stood gazing down into the pool, as though watching for an unwary trout to drift into shallow water, the trapper would soon have moved on; had he gone down to the pool for a drink it would have had the same effect.

But he did none of these things. He paused for a moment gazing down into the valley; then turned and entered the burrow but, in that one moment, he had realized what was the one thing needful to make the habitation complete. that thing was a *back door*.

Where the incline of the tunnel brought it the closest to the surface of the earth the King began excavating again, at almost a right angle to the passageway and at a steeper elevation than the other rise. He was but a few feet below the surface and, had he chosen to dig straight up, could have opened a passage to the outer world in less than an hour, but he preferred an easy grade. He dug energetically and, after a time, his mate left the bed and joined him in the work, whereupon he resumed his former occupation and removed the loose dirt as fast as she dislodged it.

When, from sheer exhaustion, the vixen ceased and crept, panting, to her nest, the King joined her. There was sand on her nose and numerous streaky patches on her sable coat but she seemed too tired to perform her customary careful toilet. Creeping closer, the King licked her face until it had again regained its velvety softness and, under the influence of that soothing touch, she fell asleep.

Suddenly the ears of the Sable King jerked forward and he became rigidly attentive. There was a faint tremor of the earth, a measured, rhythmic beat, steadily coming nearer and, in that moment, something in the consciousness of the fox recalled McElwood and the resounding tread of his feet as he walked down the lane between those little yards in the olden days.

Steadily the footsteps advanced and, in her sleep, the vixen heard. Instantly she was awake and her sharp ears twitched as she turned to face the sound. Nearer still it came and there was a certain, purposeful expression in that resounding tread that caused the foxes to shrink, tremblingly, together. At the mouth of the tunnel the steps ceased, while in the little chamber breathing almost did likewise and the blood surged afresh through the tired bodies under the impulses of their fast beating hearts.

Suddenly the silence was broken, rudely broken. A voice, a pleased, triumphant voice spoke directly into the mouth of the burrow and, in that confined space, it magnified itself until it was well nigh unbearable.

"Hello, Meestair Fox, twice times," it roared. "Dis feller, she's Pierre Laroux, de Frenchmans w'ats dam' fool for set trap. Me, I'm back on thees plac' for mak' leetle call wit' you. I'm t'ink I ain't see you much w'ile I stop on your co'ntry so I come on your house for veesit. Mebbe you com' out for see me, eh? I'm feel for shak' hand wit' you. Wat's trobble you don' com' out for get acquaint? Dat pretty poor way for treat feller w'at walk long tam for see you. Mebbe you on other side of house an' ain't hear w'at I say. P'raps I better mak' leetle smok' for call you out, eh?"

The booming voice ceased. Within the tunnel there was a trembling silence and, in that silence, the trapped foxes distinctly heard the sound of retreating footsteps. Up the bank they climbed, passed overhead and steadily receded. When they could no longer be heard the King crept to the mouth of the tunnel. Not quite to the mouth however, for a canvas bag partly obstructed the opening and that bag fairly reeked with the smell of man. He retreated hastily and, when he had reached the opening of his new tunnel, he entered and began digging furiously. This time he dug *straight up*.

A deadly fear was on him; the inherited fear of man, and this fear lent energy to his scratching forepaws and to the sturdy thrust of his hind legs as he drove the earth backward in a steady shower. For a few minutes he dug and then his ear caught the sound of those hated footfalls. Instantly he ceased digging and returned to the chamber where his mate crowded against him in terror.

Relentlessly the steps came on, hurrying slightly, and the trapped animals trembled anew, but when they again paused at the mouth of the tunnel the King crept forward, a little beyond the bend, that he might see what this fearsome creature was doing.

He was engaged in pushing a handful of dry twigs into the mouth of the hole and, when they were arranged to his liking, he covered them with dry, rotted wood and a handful of wet leaves. In the silence, the fox could hear his breathing as he bent to his task and then a new sound caught his attention; a faint scratching, accompanied by the sibilant, slithering hiss of falling sand. The vixen was in the new tunnel, digging swiftly upward toward the waning sunlight, the open air—and freedom.

[54]

Even as he started back to her assistance, there came the flare of a match and the snapping sputter of ignited wood as it was applied to the tinder. It glowed brilliantly for a moment, then died and a wisp of grey smoke bellied upward from it. Then, something that excluded the light was thrown over the opening and, save for the dull glow of the smoking wood, the tunnel was in darkness.

Again to his ears came the sound of falling sand. The vixen was digging in frenzied haste and he once more moved to help her but, as he turned in the tunnel, another odor assailed his nostrils; an acrid, tingling smell that irritated the sensitive nose as no other odor had ever done. It was the smell of smoke.

At the crucial test when Death's skeleton fingers reach out to touch a denizen of the wilds that creature, if given the faintest semblance of a chance, rises, physically at least, to sublime heights. No craven shrinking then; no cowering in a trembling ecstasy of fear as the Grim Reaper hovers closer. Then every nerve center, each muscle and sinew respond in one last, glorious, outburst of unexpected strength.

In such a manner the vixen bored upward and snarled fiercely at a bit of shale which, for a moment, retarded her progress. In such a manner, too, the Sable King labored behind her, his flying feet scooping back the sand in a never ending shower that sprayed the walls and floors of the cozy chamber which was, so soon, to have teemed with vibrant, pulsing life.

For a few minutes he kept the passage clear, then the pile of earth gradually grew higher before him. He did not realize it but those muscular legs had lost a large part of their energy. There was a biting pain in his lungs and his eyes and nose smarted horribly. He paused, involuntarily, to sneeze and then he coughed, a hollow, racking cough that brought no relief. Dimly he was aware that the sand pile before him had assumed gigantic proportions. There was a barely perceptible opening between it and the low roof of the tunnel and through this opening the smoke had not yet penetrated. On the other side he could hear his mate digging steadily on. Summoning his last reserve of strength he strove to enlarge that opening and he made headway for a few moments. Then, suddenly, his legs gave away beneath him and he fell heavily. He tried to rise but could not; his tortured lungs were crying in a rattling wheeze for air in that Hell Hole where air was not.

There was yet one minute of life in the King's glorious body and in that last minute he strove to reach his mate. He could not rise, the sight had gone from his eyes and his sense of smell had long since departed. He had no sense of direction but he writhed on the ground, and, writhing,

moved. In spasmodic jerks his legs straightened, and, foot by foot, his body moved forward. The way seemed interminably long, but still that insensate body moved on and on across the cool, damp earth: over coals that burned through hair and skin to the very flesh and, burning, brought no reflex to the spent nerves. On and on—into something soft and yielding that enveloped him as he pushed it outward from the mouth of the tunnel and let the pure, sweet oxygen surge around him in a delicious, eddying swirl. He gasped, chokingly, several times as he expelled the smoke from his laboring lungs, then the twitching muscles relaxed and, for a time, came oblivion.

Out of the black void of that unconsciousness, which was so closely allied with death, the Sable King was aware of a voice speaking; a faint, faraway voice that steadily increased in volume until it once more assumed startling proportions. He tried to rise but the stout canvas bag, with the opening drawn firmly about his neck, restrained him and he was forced to listen to the gloating Frenchman.

"W'at you t'ink of Pierre Laroux now, eh? P'raps now you ain't t'ink he's such a fool w'at he look. You needn't be scare. Pierre ain't go for kill you. Dat be dam' fool for sure. I'm go'n' wait on this plac' till dat Madame Fox he com' out; den I mak' collar an' lead you two fox out on tradin' Pos'. Fi' t'ousan' dollar they pay or I tak' you down on those United State. Ho—Ho! Pierre, he rich man, t'ank *you*, Meestair Fox."

The voice rolled on and on but the King did not heed it. A sound had come to his sensitive ears, a faint almost imperceptible sound, as of earth caving inward. The man's ears could not detect it but the fox heard it plainly and he listened eagerly.

For a moment the booming voice was silent and, in that moment, the King distinctly heard the swift patter of flying feet rapidly receding into the distance. He listened until his ear could detect it no longer. Then he slowly filled his lungs with the clear, crisp air and, as slowly expelled it. Curiously the lingering exhalation sounded remarkably like the sigh a human might emit when a soul crushing burden had been miraculously lifted.

A PAIR OF KINGS

IT was in August that McElwood received a telegram from Vancouver. It was signed by the fat director and stated, with admirable clarity, that a fox was being shipped from there, by plane, to the Maine State Fox Farms.

"Careful. Valuable." The appended warning brought a flash of color to the Irishman's watery blue eyes.

"For why, now, couldn't he be a bit careful himself," he inquired of the empty kitchen. "Here he is, runnin' from hell to Halifax lookin' for a fox to take the place of the King and bombardin' me with the craytures from ivery point of the compass. Sure it's sivin of them he's sent already and it's the divil's own time I'm havin' wit' them; the poor, wild little things. It's the death of me they'll be before I tame them—if I live that long."

From the space beneath the kitchen sink he drew forth his meticulously scoured frying pan and placed it on the polished stove. He fried a half dozen strips of bacon to an appetizing golden brown, then dropped three eggs into the smoking fat, continuing the while to deprecate his existence.

"It's several kinds of a dom fool I am to stand it," he said. "Sure, the worry of it has worn me down to skin and bones and me appetite is that small it's ashamed I am to be related to it. For why, now, don't I pack me bag and buy me a passage back to the ould sod where a little black eyed mavourneen is waitin' for me. It's a mind to do that, I have. To put on me best clothes and me best manners and say to the owners, not forgettin' to be a gentleman the whilst, 'Here's the key to your domned fox farm. Take it and go to hell wid it. It's through I am.' "

But despite his ever increasing homesickness, McElwood was still on the job when, two days later, he was informed, by telephone, that a fox had just been received by the local express office.

"As if that would make me happy," he growled into the transmitter. "It's so overworked I am, already, that I'm three days behind with me night's sleep. Not that it's any fault of yours, or that ye are carin' a whoop, me bhoy. I'll be down there directly."

He strode out to the garage, cranked the battered old flivver, climbed in and, with wide open throttle, roared out over the little lane that intersected the dirt road which led to town.

For months he had been doing, each day, what would have been a good day's work for two men. His pace had been accelerated to such a degree that haste now seemed imperative, yet he slowed the flivver to a crawl as he neared the crest of the hill that reared itself above the little town.

Shaking and shivering in every joint, as he used both brakes and the reverse pedal, the battered old car started down the precipitous descent.

"The gizzard will be droppin' out of ye on this hill some day, old girl, together with your lungs and liver," he addressed the laboring machine, "and, when it does, they'll be after shippin' me back to ould Ireland in a tomato can."

Complainingly, creaking in every straining part, the little car negotiated the perilous descent safely and the Irishman breathed a sigh of relief as he released the brakes and coasted down to the express office.

"It's down here we are," he told the express agent, "but I wouldn't take the short end of any bet that we'll get back to the top of that hill again. Where's that domned fox?"

"You're not as respectful as you might be if you knew the *domned fox* was insured for $10,000. If you ask me, that's real money, even at its present value."

"There's wan born ivry minut." McElwood's loyalty to his employers was unquestionable but his untamed Irish spirit reserved the right to criticize their actions wherever and whenever he chose.

"I niver saw but one fox that was worth the half of it— but he was the bright bhoy, and he wint where his heart was callin'."

[61]

"That was the Sable King, eh?"

"Right ye are. I'd give ten dollars to see him this minut and twenty to know he was alive and so far north that no wan would iver see him again. I liked that bhoy."

With that the Irishman heaved a tremulous sigh, acknowledged by his signature the receipt of one fox, crated, placed the crate in his car without giving its occupant more than a cursory glance, and drove off with his customary haste.

At the main gate of the outer enclosure he killed the steaming motor and lifted the crate from the car. The midsummer sun rode high in the heavens and its rays penetrated the closely slatted crate. Inside it the fox moved and a sunbeam flickered, momentarily, on a bit of his lustrous fur.

Instantly McElwood deposited the crate on the ground and was on his knees beside it, peering in at the animal.

"Sure, it's the beautiful crayture that ye are," he crooned. "You're furred enough like the King to be his own brother. Divil a bit did I think I'd ever see another wan like him. Hould your breath a minut and I'll be after havin' ye out of that box and a bit of good horse meat inside ye. It's cramped and starved and tired ye must be, poor feller, but I can remedy that. Hould everything! We're goin' inside."

He unlocked the padlocked gate, opened it, shouldered the crate and entered the enclosure. The gate swung shut behind him and he heard the patent fastening click as the bolt shot home. He entered the inner enclosure and followed the first lane over to the yard where once the Sable King had been confined. Lifting the latch he entered and eased the crate to the ground.

"This was the King's," he addressed the occupant of the box, "and a hell of a kingdom it was if you're askin' me. Such as it is, however, it's yours; renovated and whitewashed and clane enough for anywan. Just a minut, me lad, and I'll have ye out where ye can stretch your legs a bit."

He removed the twisted wire which secured the sliding door, drew that from the grooves and stepped back. Calmly and without fear the fox walked forth and stood facing the staring Irishman. The mouth of that individual slowly opened while his eyes protruded in unbelieving wonder.

"Holy Mother!" he gasped, at last. "If it isn't the King himself, I'll eat a three pound sirloin steak for me dinner on Friday."

It was the Sable King. Gaunt and far from his erstwhile immaculateness, because of the confining crate, there was yet a regalness in his carriage, a lustrous softness in his roughened coat that were unmistakable evidence in the eyes of the delighted Irishman. He knew the fox as surely as he would have recognized his old mother.

"King!" he said. "King, me bhoy! It's domned sorry I am to be seein' ye, and yet I'm that glad I could cry as aisy as a crocodile. How did it happen? Somebody played a dirty trick on ye, I'm bettin'. Ye'd never be puttin' that foot of yours in another trap, ye poor, starved little feller."

The fox regarded him gravely for a moment and there was no trace of fear in his unwinking eyes. Then he turned and walked over to his old food dish and sniffed it eagerly. With that gesture, McElwood was, immediately, his efficient self again.

"Hould tight for a minute, me lad, and I'll be back here with enough juicy red meat to twice fill the shriveled belly of ye," he said, and departed at a brisk run.

He was back, almost instantly, with a feed pail half filled with finely chopped meat and, for the first time since Pierre Laroux had smoked him from his den, the King ate with relish. Closely confined and constantly moved about, listless and uncaring he had, hitherto, eaten merely to sustain life, but now that he was once more in that environment on which his newly opened eyes had first gazed, he experienced a sense of security and wellbeing.

He had not, as yet, sworn fealty to man. A thousand generations of his progeny must know birth—and death—

in captivity before that metamorphosis should be accomplished but, in him, the first blind step toward that end had been taken. He was still a creature of the wild. He would always be exactly that but, within the confines of the yard, he was a wild thing that did not fear man.

Before he had tasted freedom he had yearned, instinctively, for the frozen arctic wastes which were his heritage. Now, that yearning was increased an hundredfold but his capable brain still kept his body under control. Around him his kindred, who had never known aught else than the restraining wires of their pens, paced restlessly, the interminable and pathetic trail that led nowhere. The Sable King ate all the succulent meat his shrunken stomach would hold, then walked over and leaped, lightly, to the flat top of the low shelter in the center of the yard.

Paying absolutely no heed to the other inmates of the farm, he turned around several times, then stretched out at full length and closed his eyelids against the glare of the summer sun. As he lay, his nose pointed, as unerringly as a magnetic needle, toward the Northland.

"How do you know it is the Sable King," asked the fat director when, some two weeks later, he stood with McElwood, looking in upon the now glistening fox.

"How do I know?" repeated the Irishman. "How do

ye know your wife and children? Do ye have to go up to them and look at a tag? Divil a bit. Ye just take a look and say 'That's me wife'—or somebody's else wife—and it's right ye are. I'm knowin' the King that same way."

"All right—all right, McElwood. I suppose you know, but whether you do or not makes little difference. He's a wonderful animal. I gave $6,500 for him at an auction and I was not the only man who wished to own him. We're going to do the New England fairs with him this fall and it will mean a whale of a lot of prestige for our farm. It's up to you to put him in the best of condition and see that he is kept that way. I suppose you were blameless over his escape last fall but—"

"Ye suppose I was blameless? I'll be after askin' ye to correct that, sir."

"Don't be touchy, McElwood. No one blamed you in the least for what happened then but it was a regrettable circumstance; very regrettable. If another accident of a similar nature occurs the company will dispense with your services. I'm telling you this in all kindness that you may practice extra precaution."

"Then how about givin' me a bit of help if you're so domned particular. Times are hard and there's many a good man would jump at the chance to work here for half what he was worth to ye. Sure, I'm that far behind—"

"Times *are* hard," the fat director interrupted. "Very hard. It's out of the question to consider hiring extra help. It's absolutely impossible."

The Irishman extracted a half dollar from his right hand trousers pocket and placed it with evident relish, in the left hand one.

"Well, it's fifty cents ahead I am, anyhow. I laid a little bet with meself this mornin' that your answer would be like that. Now, that's settled, satisfactorily, how about a dacent truck to handle the shippin'? The ould tin can has rolled moighty near her last mile, I'm thinkin'."

"Nonsense," scoffed the director. "They never wear out. Go over it in your spare time; overhaul the motor, tighten up the body bolts and it will be as good as new."

Slowly McElwood withdrew the half dollar and re-pocketed it on the right hand side. "Aven again," he said cheerfully. "I did think ye'd do somethin' about the truck. Overhaul it, did ye say? Sure, if I iver put a wrench on that wreck and gave one healthy pull, it would roll up like a window shade. There's a shipment of meat comin', sir, and I'm tellin' ye the ould girl is in no condition to handle it. What would ye be afther havin' me do? Pack it up on me back?"

"Oh, fix the truck. There can't be much wrong with it. How old is it, anyway?"

"Hivin only knows, sir. It's only thirty-two I am, me-self, and it's poorly qualified I am to judge."

"We can't purchase a new truck now, McElwood. That's out of the question. When conditions are better we will consider the matter. In the meantime, fix it up. You can do it easily enough."

"All right, sir," said the Irishman. "Although I must confess it's a bit of a disappointment. I had planned to get a few minutes sleep some night this week."

There was a hint of frost in the air. It was September and the Sable King was groomed and ready for his conquest of the New England fairs. There would be many contestants, for silver fox farms are numerous in Northern New England, but McElwood was serenely sure of the outcome.

"Sure, there isn't another fox in the wide world that could even be entered in your class, me bhoy," he told the King as he watched him lick the last succulent shreds of meat from his dish. "Not another one, anywhere, that's fit to be mentioned in the same breath with ye."

Now McElwood was Irish from his carroty hair to the soles of his generous feet and possessed the vivid imagination that was his racial heritage, but he was not clairvoyant. He could not know that, at that very moment, the King was thinking of the bewitching vixen whose regalness of carriage was equal to his own, and whose velvety coat matched his, hair for gleaming hair.

Neither could the King know that three animated replicas of himself were being schooled in the science of woodcraft, by that wise young mother.

"Yes, sir," continued the homesick Celt. "It's a prize winner ye are, and the office of the directors will be plastered with the blue ribbons ye win, but sorry consolation that will be to either of us. It's a hell of an existence for the likes of your kind and worse than that for me. You're under lock and key and can't get away, but I'm free, white and twenty-one. Why I don't pack me extra socks and beat it, I can't understand. Sure, I was ready to quit when ye was born, and it's sorry I am I didn't do it. But there was somethin' about the beautiful body of ye that kept me stayin' on, and after ye were gone, I kept thinkin' I might hear from ye. Then, when I was ready to hand over the key, ye had to come back again. Sure, ye've been the bane of my life and I hate ye for it, ye beautiful crayture. There's somethin' about ye, that houlds me, and I can't be lavin' the place whilst you're in it. Why can't ye jump the domned fences and beat it again?"

It was not given to the King to know the meaning of the words which rolled, with such a delicious brogue, from the lips of the Irishman, but he longed to be far, far from

[69]

any restraining fence. There was a mere suspicion of north wind blowing; a vagrant breeze ruffled the glistening tips of his wondrous coat and the cool tang of it was in his nostrils. With every fiber of his being he yearned for that paradise from which he was forever barred.

"There's one thing that's certain," said McElwood, "and it is this. If I get ye aboard that 9:40 train I'll have to be puttin' one foot forninst the other. Get into that box ye black beauty. Go on, with ye. Get in there. We haven't a minute to spare."

With his feed bucket he guided the fox into the open crate, closed the sliding door, shouldered the box and carried it outside the yard to the waiting flivver, and, a few seconds later, was roaring out through the little lane at his customary breakneck pace.

As he neared the crest of the hill the noise of a distant whistle reached his ears above the rattle and creaking of the old car.

"Hould tight," he flung back over his shoulder in the direction of the fox. "That's the 9:40 whistlin' the crossin' and it's down the toboggan we're goin'. Hould tight."

They pitched over the brow of the hill, and rocketed downward. Disaster almost claimed them as a front wheel dropped into a washout and in the resulting swerve they missed a boulder by inches, but with a wild "Hurro" the

Irishman swung back toward the center of the road and applied the brake slightly, for a curve and sharper descent lay just ahead.

Again the car lurched to the right, and as McElwood swung the wheel to straighten their course, it spun uselessly.

"Steerin' gear gone!" he thought even as his lips formed the words "Saint Christopher protect—"

There came a soul stirring crash, a soaring flight over jagged rocks which lined the roadside, a sickening pain in his shoulder, a desperate and ineffectual effort to regain his breath—and darkness.

It was the heat that aroused him. Fierce, scorching heat that beat down upon his upturned face and crisped the reddish hair of his eyebrows. He opened his eyes and, for one agonizing moment, while his brain struggled for mastery over the kindly oblivion which had engulfed him, he had no slightest doubt that this roaring, seething flame which leaped and twisted above him was Purgatory.

He sought to cross himself and the excruciating pain in his shoulder brought reason back. A leaping tongue of flame reached for him and, panic stricken, he tried to get to his feet, but his right arm doubled under him and his left leg seemed numb and lifeless. Determinedly he rolled over, and as his weight came down on his broken shoulder, he groaned in agony. But the relentless flame knew no mercy

[71]

and he rolled over again and again until the heat lost its power to harm.

His left arm still functioned and by its aid he achieved a sitting posture. There was a cut across his forehead and the blood blinded him. He wiped it away with his good hand and looked about. The battered car had run its last mile. It lay on its side, against the rocky bank, and roaring flame engulfed it. On the bank behind it, but so close that the slats were beginning to char, lay the crate which contained the Sable King. Crouched in the further corner, his glorious body receiving but scant protection, because of the open nature of the crate, the King faced the last Great Enemy. No living creature can look upon fire without fear, but unconquerable spirits have looked upon it without blanching. Of such fiber was the King. Within the confines of his cage, with escape cut off, he faced the holocaust with alert, clear eyes and unwhimpering lips.

Twenty feet from it the Irishman, with blood-dimmed eyes, took in the scene. It was impossible for him to make that intervening distance. Broken, wracked by tortures of the flesh that made the next breath seem an impossibility, the thing was beyond human endeavor.

Oh! God bless the Irish! The fighting Irish who accept the challenge of the Grim Reaper and leap into battle with a song in their hearts.

McElwood made it. Inch by inch—foot after agonizing foot he made it—'till at last his good left arm touched the crate. He drew himself up beside it, fell across it and wrenched a slat loose with one frenzied tug. With that as a pry he loosened another, reached in through the ample orifice and grasped the King by the skin on his neck. He drew him through the opening and flung him away from the inferno toward the lifegiving coolness behind him.

"Get the hell out of here, me bhoy," he said, weakly, and slumped across the smoldering crate.

A minute later brakes squealed as they clamped down on spinning wheels. Gravel hissed under generous tires as a high priced car came to a tumultuous halt.

The fat director emerged, followed quickly by his chauffeur. The director proved the aptness of his title.

"Man there by the wreck," he said, backing away a trifle from the fierce flames. "Drag him out, George."

George, with head bent low, accomplished it and deposited the unconscious Irishman on the bank some fifty feet from the burning car.

"Is he dead?" The director's voice expressed only mild concern.

The chauffeur eased the man over on his back and felt for heart beats. The director, looking down on that gory face, somehow recognized it.

[73]

"It's McElwood!" he shouted. "McElwood! Is he dead?"

The chauffeur said, "No. His heart is strong, sir. If you could spare him a little of your— if we could give him a drink—"

"Of course," the director said and passed over his pocket flask. George took it and poured a little between the tightly clenched teeth. A moment later McElwood stirred and rolled his head weakly, whereupon the chauffeur steadied it and held the flask to the colorless lips. As the fiery liquid touched his tongue, McElwood, true to the habits of his short lifetime, swallowed—and almost immediately opened his eyes. He ran an inquiring tongue around his lips and a little, inquisitive, sucking sound issued from them. He looked at the chauffeur and at the flask in his hand. His lips moved.

"No bird can fly properly with one wing," he whispered.

George again placed the bottle to the Irishman's lips and tilted it to his liking.

"The Sable King!" said the director, presently. "You got him to the station, did you not?"

"You're right, sor," the Irishman said and his voice lacked but little of its accustomed richness. "I did not."

"What! Where is he?"

"And how should the likes of me know. Your domned truck fell apart—your domned crate busted—and your domned fox—how should I be knowin'?"

"McElwood!" The director's voice was thin and crisp. "You are fired. Do you understand? Fired."

McElwood rolled his body slightly, got his one good elbow under him, and struggled to a sitting posture. One eye was rapidly closing but with the other he coolly surveyed the choleric fat one.

"Spheakin' as one gintleman to another," he said, "and me tippin' me hat to ye and sayin' 'Sor,' will ye kindly and politely go to hell! It's quit ye, I have, already."

JUSTICE

LUKE DODGE straightened his aching back, threw down the sickle with which he had been reaping his frost bitten corn, and struck off across the fields toward home.

"I expect it's just another one of my fool notions," he muttered as he strode along through the ankle deep grass which, despite the frosts, still retained its summer greenness. "Yes, sir, I reckon I'm being a plain, dumb fool, but," he grinned cheerfully, "it ain't the first time." Stooping, he plucked a graying straw from the green carpet and chewed it reflectively. "I've been thinking about him all morning and I might just as well drive up there and find out."

The barn, brave in its coating of red lead, stood between him and the white painted house. When he reached it he went in, cranked his battered old car and drove around to the kitchen door. There he shut off the ignition, whereupon the nondescript vehicle shivered mightily, emitted a despairing cough and subsided.

Coincident with its last spasmodic shudder, his wife appeared in the doorway. She was inclined to stoutness. As she stood there, with hands thrust into her plump hips she filled most of the opening. An aggressive figure—but her blue eyes twinkled with inborn good humor.

"Now what?" she demanded. "I s'pose you heard a pa'tridge drumming. First good day we've had this week, and you're going hunting. How and when do you ever expect to get this farm work done, I'd like to know?"

Luke's white teeth gleamed momentarily. "Aw, shucks now, Emmy, I ain't going hunting; that is, not especially. I woke up thinking about old Bennett and I ain't been able to get him out of my mind since." He opened a squealing door, climbed out and came up to the steps. "I'm going up there and see if he's all right."

Emmy surveyed him shrewdly. "I wonder, now, just what you have been thinking," she mused. "I'll bet when you woke up this morning you said, 'Gosh! There must have been a rattling good frost last night. I bet the woodcock flight was heavy, especially up in that cover of Bennett's. I'd like to be up there, after the dew is off the bushes.' Now isn't that what you thought, Luke? Honest, now, isn't it?"

"Well, maybe," Luke chuckled, then became instantly sober. "But I've been thinking about Bennett all the morning. You know how I am that way. I'm afraid something's wrong up there."

"Oh, all right, Luke, all right. Go on and have a good time. Get your gun and your shells and your hunting shoes and go up there and poke around with your old crony if you want to. I'll put up a lunch for you, and, if you'll be careful of it, I'll put in a hot apple pie for Mr. Bennett."

She bustled back to the kitchen while Luke rummaged in the hall for his hunting equipment, grinning sheepishly as Emmy muttered audible comments concerning people addicted to "spells."

Luke's movements always appeared unhurried, yet five minutes later, he was clothed in his hunting togs, had sorted out a dozen bird loads from the miscellaneous collection in his shell box, had given his prized old double gun a swift polishing with an oiled rag, and met Emmy in the pantry doorway as she emerged with the paper wrapped pie.

"Bennett'll be mighty tickled with that," he told her. "Ain't another woman 'round here can make an apple pie to compare with yours, he says."

"Why not take the applesauce up to him and leave the pie here? It's all right, Luke. You don't have to tell me white lies just to ease your conscience. Go on and have a good time."

Luke grinned and kissed her. "Know me pretty well, don't you, honey? But he did say so, really. He's a good old scout, Bennett is, and he does like your cooking." He added, maliciously, "Prob'ly I'd like it, too, if I was baching it same as he is."

"You eat enough of it, anyway," Emmy said as she

placed the pie in his hands. "Don't turn it upside down, now. That's the top. Drive careful so's to keep it right side up. Good bye."

Luke said, "Bye," tucked the pie under one arm and the shotgun under the other, went out to the car, and, with due consideraton for the pie, drove the three miles of winding road that led up to Bennett's isolated farm.

The alders brushed the sides of the car and the wheel ruts were deeply worn, but Luke steered abstractedly while his thoughts outdistanced the noisy machine. "It's just a fool notion," he said, to reassure himself. "Still, it wasn't a fool notion that time the well caved in on Lish Tabor—or the time the tree fell on Abner Berry. And I knew about Pink Bragdon and Newry—and old Mis' Chester before anyone else. Prob'ly Bennett's thinking about me for some reason or other. That's the answer. Thought transference. Yeah, that's it. He's thinking about me."

Buoyed up by this conclusion he drove into Bennett's yard and looked about. The door of the weather-beaten old house was open and swung idly in the vagrant breeze but there was no sign of life within. It was strange, Luke thought, how quiet an old house could be at times.

With a growing sense of oppression he got down from the still bubbling car and went up to the house. He put his head in the doorway and surveyed the empty room. Then, although he expected no answer, he called a cherry "Hi, there!" and waited long for an answer ere he turned and went out to the woodshed.

"Hey, Buck!" he said, as he rattled the rusty latch. "It's me, Buck." He listened for the big pointer's sniff of verification but all was silent within. Then, after a moment, for Buck was a dog with whom few liberties could be taken when he was left on guard, he swung the door wide. Save for a few low tiers of dusty birch in a far corner, the building was empty.

Closing the door he turned and surveyed the immediate surroundings—the weed grown cellar with its charred sills, where the old barn had burned last summer, the poorly kept garden with the rows of corn gray and lifeless from the recent frosts, the unmown fields with the little clumps of birches creeping in—but no sign of Bennett.

"He's prob'ly taken Buck and gone up to the cover after woodcock," Luke reflected, and knew that he was wrong. Bennett did not hunt unless he had guests. Sleek clothed, putteed chaps from the city, who knew the worth of that hillside cover and were willing to pay handsomely to hunt it behind Bennett's phenomenal pointer.

"Well, likely he's got a bunch of sports in here now," he argued, defensively, and again knew he was in error as he recalled the absence of cars in the yard.

"Buck must be around somewhere. He never leaves the farm unless he goes with Bennett." He raised his voice and called "Buck!" He listened a moment, then called again, "Here, Buck!" and watched the fringe of trees hopefully, for the appearance of that glorious liver and white pointer.

"A grand dog," he thought, as he waited. "No man ever had a better one. He knows birds, and he knows his place and keeps it." He chuckled as he thought how carefully he had announced himself at the woodshed door. "Yes, sir, he keeps his place and expects others to do the same. He's a mighty fine dog."

He waited another minute, then took his gun from the car, slid it under his arm and struck off across the field toward the birch covered sidehill.

It was singular to note the change in him now. From the time he had straightened his aching back in the cornfield at home, he had been hesitant, uncertain, seemingly half ashamed. Now he walked briskly, with determination, like a man with a preconceived plan.

Entering the woods, he continued that straight line of march until he reached what he judged to be the center of that mile long strip. There he paused. A soft breeze whispered among the almost leafless birches and stirred the brown carpet at his feet. There was no other sound.

His next action was significant of the mood that was on

him. He threw back his head and called "Hey, Buck!" Another would have said, "Hi, Bennett!" Luke Dodge called, "Hey, Buck!"

Down the wind, from straight ahead, came his answer. A piteous, whining cry.

"I knew it," said Luke. With his gun barrel he pushed aside a hindering limb and forged ahead.

Bennett lay where he had fallen, face down, among the autumn leaves, his head almost severed by a charge of bird shot that had entered his throat at close range. Buck lay beside him, his head resting on the dead man's shoulder, and a look of agony in his soft brown eyes.

"Buck!" Luke was not surprised at finding Bennett thus but he had not thought of Buck. He crouched above him and his steady hand went out slowly to caress the dog's head. "What's the matter, boy? What happened? Did they get you, too? Let old Doctor Fixit see. Atta boy."

The dog's hind legs were broken but, otherwise, he was unhurt. Luke removed his worn shooting coat and spread it on the ground. Then, as gently as he could, for Buck was a heavy dog, he rolled him upon the garment and dragged him to one side ere he gave his attention to the man who had been his friend.

Bennett, he judged, had been dead for several hours; since morning, undoubtedly, for the body was quite cold.

The twin barrels of a shotgun, which Luke knew to be the property of the dead man, protruded half their length from beneath the body. He surmised that Bennett's right hand, bent under him, still grasped the stock.

Had that weapon been discharged? Luke wondered. He knew he should not move the body. He pondered the matter for a moment, then wrapped a fold of his handkerchief about his little finger and inserted it in the muzzle of the barrels, one after the other. He studied the unstained bit of linen long and thoughtfully ere he stuffed it back in his pocket.

"That's what I thought," he said, then. "It's murder."

"I hope you'll forgive me, Buck, for not paying more attention to you," he said, later, to the dog who lay and watched him with troubled eyes. "I'll get help for you just as quick as I can, but anything we find out now may be important. You'll have to stand it a few minutes more; 'ats a good dog."

Thumb and forefinger pinching his lower lip, a deep furrow in his forehead and a pucker about his eyes, Luke Dodge pondered even as he muttered to himself.

"Shot in front—and fell forward. That means he died instantly—no turning about. Who ever did it must have stood over there, somewhere. I'll look around."

LYNN
BOGUE
HUNT

Stepping carefully, scanning the brown leaves before him, he walked several steps in the direction he had indicated, and stopped. At his feet lay two, empty, twelve gauge shells, the brave red of their paper bodies as fresh as those from a newly opened box; their high, brass bases untarnished by either rain or dew.

"Springfield Leaders!" Luke recognized the make instantly. "Their best grade. Hm-m-m—well—that's all, I guess, for now. Buck, you and me are going to notify the coroner and then hunt up a doctor for you. A good doctor, too, Buck. You bet your life on that."

Doctor Bowen was just coming down over his brick steps when Luke drew up before them in his old flivver.

"You don't have to go out looking for work, Doc," he hailed as he climbed briskly down, "for I've got a job here that will last you a spell. This dog needs attention."

"I am not a veterinary," snapped the doctor. "The animal hospital is on Third Street."

Luke gathered Buck in his arms. "I know that, Doc. I also happen to know that you are the best doctor in town. That's why we came here. This isn't just an ordinary dog, Doc. There's been a murder committed and the dog may be a valuable witness. I guess the State'll pay your bill but, if they don't you can look to me for it."

"A murder? Who was it?"

"Old Bennett, up on the ridge."

"Bennett! And this is his dog, Buck?" The doctor's voice was animated now. "Why, I've shot over him several times. A wonderful dog; wonderful. Bring him in. I'll do what I can, of course." He led the way into the house and Luke followed, bearing the unwhimpering pointer. The doctor hastily cleared his operating table and Luke laid the dog upon it.

"Now, Buck," he said then, "I've got to leave you. The coroner's waiting for me. I'm sorry to quit you now but Doc, here, is a friend of yours. He'll fix you up all right. You understand, don't you, old fellow?"

Buck's brown eyes watched Luke as he crossed the room and passed through the open door. Then his head swung slowly until his gaze rested on the doctor, who, with sleeves rolled up, was busily sorting instruments.

Soft eyes? Yes. Uncomplaining eyes? Yes. Understanding eyes? Yes.

"The way I figger it," Luke explained to the coroner as they stood looking down at the body, "Bennett was murdered. The fellow that shot him was a bird hunter and a good one. He—"

"Explain that, will you, Luke? How do you know he

was a bird hunter, and, more especially, how do you know he was a good one?"

"I picked some shot out of Buck's leg," Luke confessed. "They were number nines. Nobody but bird hunters, and mighty few of them, use nines. Most amateurs think they're too small. This fellow knew they were big enough for pa'tridge and woodcock when they were near. If he could hit 'em when they were close he was a good shot. He used high grade shells, knowing by experience that they were better. There's the empties over by that bush. He didn't know when he threw them out. If you don't believe that, go ask any experienced shooter. He'll tell you he loads his gun unconsciously after shooting it."

"It sounds plausible, Luke. You have some idea how it happened. Reconstruct it for me, will you?"

"I've been thinking it over," Luke said, "and the way I dope it out, Bennett heard someone shooting up here early this morning. You know that this cover and his trout pools are about the only way he had of earning a living. City sports paid him a mighty nice price for the privilege of hunting this sidehill and fishing his pools. Of course he was anxious to protect the birds, so when he heard the shooting, he grabbed his gun, called Buck, and beat it up here hot footed. When he found the chap he probably threatened to have him arrested. They argued, each gettin' madder all the time, and then this feller made a threatening move toward Bennett. When he did that, Buck jumped for him. He was a fast man. He snapped the gun up, centered the dog, and pulled the trigger as quick as you could wink an eye. But the dog was going up in his leap, and his hind legs were down from their drive. The charge passed under his body but got him in both hind legs, breaking the bones.

"Then, out of the tail of his eye, this feller seen Bennett swinging his gun up and he beat him to it. I'll bet them two shots were quicker'n you could snap your fingers twice. He stopped a minute, looking to see what he'd done, and loaded his gun while he stood there. Then he beat it. That's the way the thing looks to me."

"Can you make a guess as to who did it?"

"No. A lot of the younger crowd didn't like him because he posted his land, but us older ones didn't blame him. It was some young chap in town, I should guess."

"And you have no idea who it was?"

"Not me," Luke answered. "No, I ain't got the slightest idea who it was—but I know someone who has."

"Who is that?"

"Buck," said Luke, grimly. "Yes, sir, you bet your life Buck knows. That's one of the reasons why I picked Doc Bowen. I didn't want to run any chances of losing our only witness."

The coroner looked at him approvingly. "For a farmer, you're not so slow, after all," he admitted.

Late that afternoon Luke's car was once more parked before the doctor's home and Luke was inside, examining the plaster casts that were hardening about Buck's legs.

"It will be necessary to keep him in a sling for several weeks, until the bone knits," the doctor told him. "I would suggest that you take him down to the animal hospital. He will require considerable attention and you will find it quite a burden to take care of him."

Luke grinned apologetically. "I've got a sort of weakness about dogs, Doc, and especially about Buck. I couldn't cart him off down there and leave him among strangers. I'll take him home, and if you'll come up once in a while and tell me what I'm doing wrong, I guess we can make out to keep him comfortable. Will you do that for us?"

"Of course. He was the best woodcock dog I ever saw. I'll look after him, and if he comes through all right, I would like to take part of my pay in shooting over him a day or two next fall."

"If he pulls through, you'll get as many days shooting over him as you care to take. Nobody ever had a better bird dog, but I'm hoping to try him out on bigger game when he gets well. You've been white, Doc."

Luke Dodge had always been a bird hunter, but shortly thereafter, he became the most enthusiastic one in town. In Brock's hardware store, at the Fish and Game Club, in the poolroom, on street corners, wherever two or more hunters assembled, there Luke could be found, asking questions and listening avidly to all conversations. It was a slow process but, in the end, he gleaned the information he coveted. There were three men in town who invariably used number nine shot.

That one of the three was the man he sought, he was thoroughly convinced, but to prove it was a different matter. With what native, inborn tact he possessed, he cultivated their acquaintance and tried to convince them of his friendship. One at a time he hunted with them, and while they rode to the covers, or ate their noonday lunch, he talked of various things, but never, by any chance, of Bennett.

Of Bennett's dog, however, he talked much. Buck, he contended, was the best dog in Strafford County. Billy Collins agreed with him. Billy had seen Buck work; had, in fact, shot over him once. Together they went into Luke's house. Billy patted Buck on the head and told him he was a good dog, and to hurry up and get well, and get them old legs mended before another fall.

Later, Speed Flynn came in and admired Buck's admirably chiseled head, bragging, the while, of pointers he had owned and trained. Buck, bored, as was Luke, yawned and rudely went to sleep ere the visitor had departed.

Nick Giles said he guessed he couldn't stop tonight. Some time, when it wasn't so late, he'd like to see him, although he didn't care much for pointers as a rule. Give him a setter, like Pete, here, every time. Oh, sure, he had heard about Buck. He guessed he was a good dog, all right but—well—he would come in for a minute.

Buck had looked at him briefly, and turned his eyes away. Only momentarily, however. They came back and rested on Giles' face. Luke, watching closely, saw the hair bristle suddenly along the dog's spine. In that instant he wished that Buck were well again. The dog made no sound, no movement other than that involuntary contraction of the skin, but the man had a presentiment that only the restraining canvas and the plaster casts prevented the dog from making a desperate try to reach the man's throat.

Buck knew. Luke knew. Nick Giles, looking deep into the dog's soul, knew.

Two hours later, Luke was closeted with the County Attorney. Painstakingly, missing no essential detail, he presented his case, and, in the end, saw the official shrug his shoulders helplessly.

"You have a clever theory, Mr. Dodge," he said, "but very little more. The only actual facts you have uncovered are that Giles prefers a certain size shot for a certain type of hunting, and that Bennett's dog dislikes him. That Bennett was killed, and his dog wounded by shot of that size, makes little difference. For all you know, a thousand men within a ten mile radius may use them occasionally. Do you expect me to put a man on trial for his life with no more evidence than that?"

"No," admitted Luke. "No, I didn't expect you would, but I wanted you to know what I'd found out. It ain't much in the way of evidence but it's probably all we'll ever get. We can't prove nothing against him, but just as sure as I'm standing here, Nick Giles killed Bennett. Buck knows. He *knows*, I tell you. You can't go behind that."

"Forget it," the attorney advised. He arose and stretched his angular frame and Luke knew the interview was over. "There are a hundred crimes committed for each conviction. Forget it. There is very little involved, anyway. Bennett had no dependents, had he?"

"No," Luke answered, slowly. "No, I guess he didn't have a relative in the world, and only a few friends, but Buck and me happen to be two of 'em. I know it ain't any use to try and prove it against Giles—but we don't forget things very quick. Yes, I reckon me and Buck will remember this for quite a spell. Well, that's all, I guess. I'll be going now. Good night, sir."

It was Christmas day when they took Buck out of the sling. The plaster cast had been off for several days and Luke had, painstakingly, taught the dog to use those lifeless legs once more.

"I never did see a dog so quick to learn, Emmy," he told his wife after the second lesson. "Look at him kick those legs, will you? Pretty near human, that dog is."

Buck, lying suspended in the sling, with his toes just touching the floor, would cease his awkward kicking to look up at them understandingly, and would then begin again—left, right, left, right—his toenails making erratic scratches on Emmy's hardwood floor.

This day they made quite a ceremony of freeing him of his last protective appliance. Doctor Bowen drove out in the early afternoon. Emmy had made a chicken pie especially for Buck, and he walked across the kitchen floor to get it. After he had eaten it the Doctor presented him with a bill for professional services. Buck regarded it gravely when it was held before him.

"That's white of you, Doc," Luke said when he saw it was marked "Paid in Full." "That's mighty white. You're due for some happy days with the woodcock next fall.

Come, Emmy, set the table. Doc's eating Christmas dinner with us."

It was a rainy April night, but sometime in the early morning hours the rain ceased and the soft stars came out. The eastern sky was just showing the faintest trace of pink when Luke stirred and opened his eyes. Somewhere in the distance he could hear a car laboring through the soft mud. It came nearer and passed the house, while he drowsily tried to recognize it by the sound of its noisy motor. Somewhere he had heard a machine exactly like that. Half awake, he pondered the matter and wondered whose it was, then decided it sounded exactly like his own, or any other worn out flivver, and went to sleep again.

Sometime later he awakened with a start. The sun was shining brightly outside and the newly arrived birds were greeting it with joyous throats. The clock on the dresser insisted it was 5:23. He got out of bed at once and began to dress.

With one foot half through his trousers leg he stopped and stood, storklike, staring into space.

"Now why," he asked of nothing in particular, "should I be thinking of Nick Giles the minute I get out of bed? Pshaw! What a dumb fool I am! That was his car I heard. Going fishing, of course."

"I thought it was about time." Emmy sat up in bed and began undoing her curling papers. "I saw some robins digging worms yesterday. When did you plan this up?"

"Honest, Emmy, I haven't planned anything up. I just happened to think of Nick Giles, that's all. I guess it must have been his car that went by in the night. It woke me up."

"I've noticed one thing in the twenty years that we've been married, and that is that you wake up awfully easy during the fishing and hunting seasons. Other times, a tornado, with thunder and lightning, wouldn't make you roll over. Are you going to try flies?"

"Flies? This early? No, I'm going to use—there, what am I saying? I ain't even thought of going fishing. I tell you I just happened to think of Nick Giles."

"Oh, yeah?" said Emmy.

Luke milked his cows, poured a quart of the warm fluid in Buck's pan, and a smaller quantity in another dish for Belinda and her three kittens. Then he opened the door leading from the tieup into the barn.

"Hey, Buck!" he called. "Your milk's getting cold. Come and get it," but Buck did not appear.

"He's out pointing robins, probably," Luke decided and went into the house with the full pails.

"Well, it looks as though spring had got here at last,

Emmy," he said, conversationally, as he entered the kitchen.

"Yes. I've been seeing signs of it all morning. Your rubber boots are hanging in the shed and your rods are in the hall cupboard. Have you dug your worms yet?"

"Quit kidding me, can't you? I told you I wasn't going fishing. I just happened to think of Giles, doggone him, up there at Bennett's private pools."

"Now don't get peevish, Luke. Why don't you go if you want to? It's too early to do much farm work, and you might just as well get some of this fishing out of your system."

Luke grinned. "Trying to get a rise from me, eh? Well, you're casting short, girlie, you're casting short. No, somehow I don't feel as though I wanted to go fishing today. I'm going out to feed the cows and hens. I'll be back in a few minutes."

Halfway across the yard he stopped suddenly, and clenched his fists. "Why, doggone his soul!" he said. "He's got a nerve to go up there. I should think, after what he did, he'd be afraid—" He looked up, quickly.

Buck was coming across the fields, from the direction of the woods, running with a free and easy stride, as a wolf runs. There was a rhythm in the play of those glorious muscles, a lightness that was surprising in a dog as heavy as he.

It seemed as though some burden that weighed him down had, suddenly, been lifted.

On he came, across the corner of the old garden, over the stone wall in one long, rainbow curve, through the yard and up to the barn door. There he stopped, looked up at Luke and parted his jaws in what the man remembered to be his old time grin.

Buck was himself again. He was well and tremendously strong, but Luke was not thinking of that. He was staring, wide eyed, at the once white throat and chest of the big pointer. It was white no longer. It was now a somber brown, not unlike Buck's liver colored saddle.

Luke looked into the big dog's face. His eyes noted the gleaming, incisor teeth. Teeth capable of cutting deep in soft flesh. Teeth that were snow white once more.

"Why, you old son-of-a-gun!" said Luke. "Come in here where I can wash that blood off you. Nobody's going to know about this, Buck. Nobody but just you and me."

NAIL," said the mechanic. "I can see the head of it. Right there, see. I can patch it or sell you a new tube for two and a quarter."

"Patch it," I said. "And make it as snappy as you can. I have another two hundred miles to do before dark."

"Yes, sir. Take about half an hour. Them damn rims —" He straightened and stared as a towing car, trailing a twisted, battered wreck, swung into the yard and came to a halt beside the garage.

"Gawd, that one has been places," the mechanic stated. I agreed with him. Apparently the machine had slid for miles on one side; both mudguards were gone and the body was scoured to a mirror brightness. If my judgment was correct it had then rolled over several times, for the top was shredded to ribbons and the rear mudguard, on the opposite side, seemed mostly elsewhere.

As it came to a halt the door opened, on squealing hinges, and a disheveled figure emerged from the interior. There was something hauntingly familiar about the man, in the indecisive manner with which he moved about the wreck and the absent-minded gesture of wiping his brow with a handkerchief which had lost much of its snowy whiteness. I approached him. He turned slightly, exposing a clean-cut profile and an aquiline nose that had been bleeding recently.

Bruised and battered as those features were I recognized them.

"Nick!" I said. "Nick Stewart! What happened?"

"Everything." His tone was flat, hopeless. "Hello, Bill. Yes, almost everything has happened and the rest is—My God! Is that you, Bill?" He advanced with outstretched hand. "Haven't seen you since—" He broke off abruptly and stared at my car as though it were a prehistoric mammal. "They told me there wasn't a car in the place. Is that yours, Bill? Thank heaven!" He grasped me by the arm and whirled me about in the direction of the car and urged me forward.

"Get in!" he shouted. "I'll drive. I can make better time than you. Got gas enough?"

"Plenty," I assured him, hanging back. "Also a flat tire. What's the main idea?"

He stopped short and the animation went from his face as though wiped off by one stroke of a giant sponge. "That settles it," he said tonelessly. "There's no hope. I've lost her!"

"Lost her?"

"Absolutely. Not a chance in the world, now. God!"

"Lost whom, Nick?"

"Alicia Wainwright." As he said it his face grew softly luminous like that of Saint Cecilia at the organ. "She'll be gone and I can never explain it to her. No hope! No hope!"

"What's the matter, Nick? Is there anything I can do?" I asked.

"Nothing, absolutely n—What did you say? Yes, of course there is. Give me a drink."

There was a half pint of Scotch in the car from which just one little nip had been taken. I gave it to him and he emptied it in three prodigious gulps, looked blankly at the empty flask for a moment, sighed and tossed it into the ditch.

"Listen, Bill," he said then. "How much experience have you had with women? Are you a married man?"

"You were one of the ushers," I reminded him.

"Was I? It had slipped my mind. Well, listen. In your experience, what do you, as a married man, think a girl would think if you—that is, if I asked her—I'm afraid I'm putting this rather badly."

"A trifle ambiguous, Nick," I admitted. "If I follow your thought, you were inquiring what I, benedict, would imagine a girl, spinster, would say if you bachelor, should ask her—what?"

He mopped his brow uncertainly. "I'm afraid that isn't it at all," he said. "I'll put it another way. Suppose you were

going to be married and something—something that wasn't
my fault in the least—"

"Your fault, or mine?"

"Eh? Well, something that wasn't in the least bit your
fault should happen so that you knew that I—you were
going to be late for the wedding. Would she—she might
not like—er, what would she say?"

"God knows, Nick. They have a great vocabulary."

"Then you think she might be a little bit—er—the
chances are about fifty-fifty she would—"

"Take the advice of a friend," I urged him, "and don't
ever become a bookmaker. If you gave odds like that you
wouldn't last long enough to—"

"Then you think—Alicia—might not like it?"

"Listen, Kid," I told him. "I don't know Alicia, but I
have passed the time of day with several members of her sex.
If you are a split second late for your wedding, she'll be so
worried that she'll fall on your neck—and break it."

"You're a pessimistic hound, Bill. Now listen to this
and see if you think I can be blamed for the things that happened. They were absolutely out of my control. Not one
thing—"

"What time is the halter supposed to be snapped around
your neck?" I interrupted. "My tire will be ready in twenty
minutes. Perhaps I can get you there in time for the—"

"Not a chance," he groaned. "We are forty miles from —it was the telegram that—No, it doesn't rightly begin there. It begins later than that. It begins at exactly four o'clock this morning. My alarm clock woke me and I lay there a minute wondering what the deuce I had set that for, and then I remembered the telegram. You can imagine how I felt, can't you, when I realized that—"

"I don't get a very clear picture of it," I said. "Slightly out of focus in the foreground and background, while the center is—"

"It seems as though you must understand that. Suppose that you had awakened an hour before dawn and felt a happy glow all over, and lay there wondering why, and then, all at once, you remembered that just before midnight you had received a telegram from Tichnor calling your attention to the fact that the next morning at nine, he was going to dispose of his entire kennels. *His entire kennels!* Do you get that? What would that do to you?"

"It would make me yawn prodigiously," I assured him. "Who is Tichnor, anyway? What has he ever done for his country?"

"My God, Bill!" For a moment I thought he was going to hit me. "Who is Tichnor? What has he ever done for his country! I'll tell you what he has done," he shouted. "He has bred more bird dogs that have taken more prizes on more courses and before more judges than any other ten men in the country. Now do you see?"

"Perfectly," I answered. "It's as clear as pea soup, now that you have explained the situation. You awaken, on your wedding morn, and recall that Ticker is selling a handful of bird dogs. Very lovely and beautifully expressed."

He regarded me gravely for a moment. "And to think," he said, "that with all our modern advantages a person could remain so—Bill! Didn't you know that I was interested in bird dogs?"

I recalled it then. Some alumnus had told me that Nick was letting the steel mills run themselves and had gone into field trial dogs in a big way.

"I believe I did hear that you had taken a passing fancy to the bird hounds," I said.

"Setters," he informed me. "The hounds are out. There isn't a pointer in my kennels."

"No?"

"Not one. There are sixty-seven as sweet setters as you ever laid eyes on in my yards, and they are at present, headed by Rodney's Count Whitestone."

"Nobility, eh?"

"I'll say so!" All at once his eyes lighted up and his face glowed with animation. "He was runner-up in the National two weeks ago. Man, oh Man! Was that a heat! Listen. The judges put them down on stubble at 10:45. Count made a mile cast and pointed before Raprap, his brace-mate, had drawn game. We rode up and—"

"What has that to do with alarm clocks?"

"What? Alarm clocks?" He looked puzzled. "Oh, yes, where was I?"

"In bed. The alarm clock was ringing. Ticker had sent a telegram saying—"

"Tichnor, not Ticker. W. Z. Tichnor. Well, as I lay there thinking, it suddenly dawned on me that here was a business opportunity I couldn't afford to pass up. I was interested in setters and, naturally, wanted the best. The kennels, as an investment, hadn't been—well—not all that I had hoped. Getting started, you know, and trying out different strains and discarding the undesirables, had run up quite a tidy little sum. Nothing extravagant, but—"

"How much to date, Nick?"

"Well, roughly, around one hundred and eighty thousand. Good trainers command a pretty fair salary, but I am getting along with only nine. The yard boys are common labor, but the cooks and dietitian draw fair wages. I pay a veterinary a flat, yearly rate and he looks the dogs over every morning. After that he is free to attend his regular practice unless—"

"How does the income stack up alongside the outgo?"

"It is considerably smaller," he said, "but still not bad. This is my first season in competition, but I took seven thirds at one hundred each and two seconds at two fifty. That's—seven and—"

"Twelve hundred."

"Exactly. Then there were three silver cups, plated, and five ribbons in the derby class and—"

"Three times $.98 is $2.94, and—Oh, call it three dollars. Twelve hundred and three dollars for receipts, and about one hundred and eighty thousand in expenditures. Not bad, not bad."

Nick beamed again. "Pretty good, eh, for the first season, but still not quite satisfactory. I suppose it was thinking of that which gave me the idea. 'Here's my chance,' I thought, 'to go down to Tichnor's and get the pick of absolutely top stuff. Nothing better in the United States—or the whole world either, for that matter. It would put my kennels right. Absolutely right.' I knew I couldn't really afford it, with business shot to hell the way it is, but if I had the stuff they would have to come to me to get it, and I could charge a stiff price and get away with it. Then, too, I thought of Alicia. I didn't at first, I'll admit, but later I did and that decided me. I would go the limit for her sake. I made up my mind I'd buy every dog Tichnor owned and put our kennels so far above the rest of them that—"

"Alicia is a—a dog fancier, then?"

"Not exactly," he confessed. "She's—well, she is a society girl and hasn't had much experience with them. In fact, she is a trifle timid about the kennels and has the worst case of gun shyness I have ever seen, but that is a fault which can be easily cured. I have a trainer who—"

"We were speaking of Alicia," I reminded him.

"Were we? Oh, yes. I was thinking—What did you do with that Scotch?"

"Practically nothing—and there isn't any more. Alicia?"

"Yes, yes, I'm coming to that. You'll have to meet her. She's a thoroughbred. Pedigree as long as—" He stopped, looked blankly around as though viewing his surroundings for the first time and resumed:

"But that is all over now. After this, she will never even look at me again. And it was not in the least my fault. You understand that, don't you, Bill?"

"Perfectly," I assured him.

"Thanks. Well, I switched the alarm off and dressed quietly, got my check book, and went out to the garage. I took the Packard—it was faster and I knew there wouldn't be much time to spare. Sweet car, that, Bill."

I glanced at it. "Lovely," I assented.

"It was nearly five when I started, but I was there before

seven. Wanted a chance to check up on his feeding system and younger stock with which I was unfamiliar. I was early, but I hadn't been there ten minutes before a car drove up and Sam Tyler got out. You know Tyler, don't you?"

"Couldn't distinguish him from Adam."

"Bill! You don't even know Tyler? Well, listen." He spoke slowly, distinctly, as though explaining something to a particularly backward child. "Tyler is head handler for Mark Little, and he placed thirty-seven dogs this season. Do you get it now?"

"I think so. Old Man Competition, eh?"

"Exactly. I didn't get it then; but when cars containing the best known bird dog men in the country kept rolling in, one after another, it—well, it dawned on me that perhaps I was not the only man Tichnor had notified. I began to feel that prices might be run up so high that I couldn't buy them all. I had about thirty thousand dollars that I could spare—not exactly surplus, you understand, but available —and, including puppies, there were exactly one hundred and eighteen dogs to be sold. So I went through the kennels again and checked up on the ones which I felt I absolutely must have. It's strange how a man can renounce an ambition when he realizes that it's—well—imperative. How many do you suppose were on my final list?"

"One hundred and seventeen?"

"Too high. No, sir. When I had scratched everything but the very choicest, there were only thirty-two on the list."

"Only thirty-two, Nick. How you must have felt!"

"Absolutely rotten, Bill. And I had started out with such high hopes. It seemed—"

"Still," I interrupted, "Thirty-two has its advantages. Added to the sixty-seven it makes a not insignificant total. You can stroll around, singing that grand old hymn: 'There were ninety and nine that safely lay in the shelter of the fold—' "

"Ghastly," he said. "Absolutely ghastly—and at a time like this. Listen, I've had about all of everything I can stand today. One more crack like that and—"

"Oh, forget it, Nick. Forgive and forget."

"I can forgive anything, but I can never forget this day, never. You can't imagine what I have been through, Bill. One disappointment after another until—well, here's a sample:

"Among many others Tichnor had one brood matron that I just had to own. She has the greatest record of any living dam. Has whelped fourteen dogs that have won thirty-nine firsts and two grand championships. She is still only seven years old and in whelp to St. Regis. I was looking at her when Tyler came up.

" 'Well, the old girl is about done for,' he said. 'Too bad. She's been a great matron, but she's had her last litter. Too bad—too bad.'

"Now Tyler is absolutely top when it comes to judging dogs and I have always had a high opinion of him, but I found out today that he is a very low type. Subsequent events proved that. Listen. Can you imagine a man, in his position, pursuing tactics that a cracker would be ashamed to practice?"

"Feeding you poison ivy, was he?"

"Absolutely. I didn't get it then, but I did later. The bitch looked in perfect condition and I was still of a mind to buy her. If he had a different opinion it was not up to me to change it and consequently shove the price up, was it?"

"I am totally unfamiliar with the ethics of dog buying," I told him. "Probably you were right."

"Certainly I was right. And they were all the same— every damn man of them. If I stopped before a certain dog some crook standing there would inform me it was coming down with distemper, or had tender feet, or that the only thing that kept it from being a bird dog was some speed and a nose to go with it. By the time the auction started I was down to just thirteen dogs, including St. Regis, Lady Landsdowne and a youngster who had taken first in the all-age up in Manitoba on chicken."

"Chicken?"

"Yes. Prairie chicken. First cousin to the ruffed grouse, and an entirely different bird to handle. I recall an incident that happened last year. I had gone up to Manitoba with a brace of dogs that were pretty well finished on quail. They were fast and wide, and I had an idea I could land something up there in the way of a trophy. A ribbon or two, or maybe a cup. Well, do you know that when we put them down the first day—"

"Nick! Is this getting us any nearer the climax of the drama?"

"I was explaining the necessary difference of method in handling a quail dog on chicken. You know the quail is a close lying bird, given to—"

"But what has this to do with the auction at Ticker's—Tichnor's—or wedding bells, for that matter?"

"Why, because—" He paused and again stared, uncomprehendingly, at me. "What? I'm afraid I was thinking of something else. Well, as I was saying, quail are customarily found in—Where was I? Oh, yes. I had started for Tichnor's and—"

"You had arrived, Nick. You had cut your prospective purchases to thirteen, and the auction had started. Now go on with the story."

"Did I mention Lady Landsdowne?"

"More than that, Nick. Some of the things you said about her actually made me blush."

"What? Well, then I must have spoken of Lord Blackstone?"

"No. I believe you attributed her downfall to Saint somebody or other."

"Regis," he said. "St. Regis. Great dog, that. Wonderful. But I was speaking of Lord Blackstone—the dog that took the chicken championship. He was the first dog put upon the block. Sort of a feeler to gauge the buying power by, I suppose. Tichnor acted as auctioneer. He is as smooth as they make them.

" 'Gentlemen,' he says, 'I am retiring. I've bred my last dog. Today I hope to dispose of them to the last pup. To tell you anything about them would be a waste of time. You know them all—or you will some day. This is Lord Blackstone. Who will start this off with a bid of one thousand dollars?'

"Honest to God, Bill, I'll bet twenty men said, 'Here,' and before Tichnor could get a chance to speak, they had run the price up to twenty-two hundred dollars. I never experienced anything like it. Do you know what he sold for finally?"

"Twenty-five hundred?"

"And one. Selwyn from Georgia quit at twenty-five

hundred, and Tyler bid another dollar and got him. They were crazy, absolutely crazy. Do you know, I believe that most of the dog men I know are really a little bit peculiar. Did you ever notice it?"

"Now that you mention it," I said, "I do recall certain instances which seemed to lend color to your observation."

"Not all of them, of course. There are a few, like Tichnor and—well—myself, who take a sane viewpoint of the game, but to illustrate: I bid two thousand on Lord Blackstone but not another penny would I go. Why? Because I knew he wasn't worth it. That proves it, doesn't it?"

"Unquestionably. And Tick—Tichnor took the two thousand, five hundred and one. He's acquitted also."

"What? Oh, yes, of course. Well, as I was saying, I saw men go crazy today. Absolutely screwy. The place was a shambles. Only by the most rigid self control did I restrain my inclination to follow suit. But I did, Bill. I let dog after dog go that I'd have given my heart to own, simply because the price went above all reason. Of course, there were exceptions. Not many; but once or twice I bid fairly high. I had to, you understand, in that bunch of maniacs."

"What did they stick you for Lady Lambsdown?"

"Landsdowne, Bill. Considering the way prices were going, I didn't pay an excessive figure. In fact, I didn't pay too high for any of those I bought, and if it hadn't been for

Tyler I'd have made a real bargain on Lady Landsdowne."

"Tyler?" I said. "He's the chap who spoke slightingly of the lady?"

"The same," Nick answered. "Strange, how I have been deceived about that fellow. Why, at one time I thought I liked him. Honestly, Bill, time after time when I had a real sweetheart of a dog as good as in my kennel, he would swing in after the others had quit, and bid him out of my reach. His manner, too, was positively insulting. As much as to say, 'Now that the *canaille* have slit each other's throats, I'll buy your dog, mister.' "

He laughed suddenly, a short harsh laugh that was utterly devoid of humor. "But he hauled in his horns on Lady Landsdowne. That was worth all it cost. For some reason or other the bidding on her was not brisk. I doubt if Tyler's remarks about her had anything to do with it, for by that time every man there must have realized he was lower than a U-boat, but the price started surprisingly low. Five hundred, I think it was, and advanced by fifties rather than the customary hundreds. It began to look as though I would get her for about fifteen hundred, and she was worth that, Bill, in any man's money.

"They quit at thirteen fifty, and I shoved it up twenty-five. Tichnor said, 'Who will make it fourteen?' and nobody spoke. 'Going,' said Tichnor. 'Going at thirteen hundred and seventy-five dollars. Going—going—' and Tyler yawned and said, 'Fifteen hundred.' Honest, Bill, that got me and I said, 'Two thousand.' Maybe I spoke rather sharply, for he looked around and grinned at me and said, 'Three.'

"I tried to match his smile. 'Four,' I said. 'Golfer, eh?' he asked. 'Forty-five hundred—and let's see you top that one.'

" 'You're cluttering up the fairway,' I told him, 'but bid your limit and then get off the course. I'm buying this dog.'

" 'Says you? Well, Nick, it isn't my money or my judgment I'm using. If it had been, you could have owned her three thousand dollars ago. I'm acting on orders. "Up to five thousand on Lady Landsdowne," says Mr. Little, so up to five thousand she goes.'

" 'Piker's money,' I told him. 'Five thousand and one.'

" 'Fool's gold,' he said. Now wasn't that uncalled for, Bill? Then some one in the crowd said, 'Gettysburg? Don't ever mention Gettysburg after this, suh. I've seen a real war.'

"All this time Tichnor had been little more than a spectator, now he spoke. 'Sold to Nick Stewart,' he said. 'And now, gentlemen, will you excuse me for a moment? I believe I need a drink,' and he went into the house.

"Several times I'd noticed a tall nigger weaving through the crowd and leading a disreputable little setter. Now, in that moment of quiet, he mounted the steps and placed the dog on the table before him. It was dirty and snippy nosed and frightened, and as it stood there with its back humped up and its tail between its legs, it was absolutely the poorest specimen I ever saw.

" 'Gemmen,' says the darkey. 'If yawl wanna buy a buhd dawg, whyn't yawl buy this Jack dawg. Cain't keep th'ee dawgs nohow an' cain't hunt 'thout cat'iges. Fust man gimme hunderd dollahs gwine own a buhd dawg. Who gwine pay me?'

" 'I'll give you ten,' said Tyler, 'if you'll deliver him to the nearest sausage factory.' Everyone laughed.

" 'Ten dollahs gwine buy a lot o' cat'iges,' said the coon. 'Boss, yo' bought yo'se'f a dawg.'

"Tyler dug in his pocket while the crowd roared. 'It's my money this time,' he said. 'Here you are, George, and hold him for me a while, will you?'

"Then Tichnor came out, and we all forgot the incident as the heavy artillery opened fire again. And was it heavy! Bill, don't let anyone tell you there is a depression. I didn't know there was so much money in the world. They were lousy with it. I——" his voice trembled and broke—"I didn't get St. Regis."

"No?"

"No. Bill, you will never know how much—but I musn't talk about it—I musn't even think about it. I had spent more than I intended on Lady Landsdowne, and had just fifty-three hundred left." He sighed. "It wasn't enough. Tyler took him at sixty-seven hundred."

"Pretty fair price," I remarked.

"Fair," said Nick. "Just fair. Oh, if I had only—but it's all over now. I'll go crazy if I—*Look at that head, will you!*"

A car had driven up to the line of pumps and was honking loudly for gas. Through the open window at the driver's right, a setter's head was thrust. Sharply outlined in black and white and framed by the rectangular opening, it made a pleasing picture. Nick strode over to the car.

"Fine looking dog, you have, brother," he said. "What's his breeding?"

"I don't know," the man answered. "He isn't registered."

Nick said, "Oh," and came, angrily, back.

"Damned shame," he said. "Imagine it! Owning a dog like that and not having his pedigree. It's criminal."

"The dog seemed happy," I suggested. "Do you suppose they care as much as you think?"

"There are no friendships so strong as those formed in college," he said. "God knows that otherwise I would have killed you long ago. If you were not absolutely dumb, you would know the value of registration. See here." He held up his left hand. "A," he said, indicating the index finger, "buys a bird dog which is stolen by B." His second finger became B. "C likes the looks of the dog, breeds to it and sells one of the litter to D. Do you grasp the situation?"

"Perfectly. The answer, of course, is X. And now let us get back to our garden sass. You missed St. Regis by more than a thousand dollars—and then you remembered this was your wedding day and you were going to be late for dinner. Is that the story?"

"Not quite," he said. "With all the excitement of the sale and arranging for the shipment of the dogs, I—I—well, Bill, I forgot it, momentarily. Several times I was on the very verge of recalling it, and then something would happen to distract my attention. After I had given Tichnor my check and arranged for a truck to convey them to my kennels, I am quite sure I would have remembered, but Selwyn came up just then and asked if I was entering the free-for-all.

" 'Where are they running it and when?' I asked him.

" 'Right here and now,' he said. 'Leighton and Crowder got into an argument as to which one had picked the best derby prospect and decided to settle it right out here on Tichnor's preserve. There are a dozen in it already.

Stake is five hundred, and winner takes all. Any dog which has never been placed is eligible. Better get in.'

"I had picked up a youngster that I had seen work this fall. Fast and wide and a great nose. He would have taken the derby but he broke point once. Nothing serious, you know. Any young dog is likely to do it in competition. He was a good bet, and here, I thought, was a chance to pick up a nice piece of change.

" 'Sure, I'm entering,' I told him. 'Where do we register?'

"He indicated a gesticulating group of men on one of the lawns. I went over. Tyler was talking. 'So why not make the stakes worth while,' he was saying. 'First dog to point game shall be the winner, and instead of a five hundred entrance fee, let the owner of the winner take all the entries. There's a chance for some one to clean up.'

"I remember thinking at the time that here was a red hot proposition. The race would not last a half hour and some one would walk off with close to fifty thousand dollars' worth of bird dogs.

" 'That's talking turkey,' I said. Then I saw a chance to get back at Tyler. 'I would suggest, however, that each man shall possess a clear title to the dog he enters. Then, if he loses, there can be no wriggling out from under.'

"I'll say that they were sportsmen, for they agreed to

it to a man. Even Tyler. 'That's a fair proposition,' he said. 'I am for it.'

"We selected Tichnor for a judge and instructed him to declare that dog a winner who should first come to a productive point. With that we started off across the fields, more than a dozen of us, each man with a setter on leash. Looking the crowd over I spotted Tyler. 'How did you get in here?' I asked him. 'Spectators are required to stay behind the judges.'

" 'I'm no spectator,' he said, and grinned. 'I'm entering my Jack dawg. You are all witnesses to the fact I personally bought this dog.'

"He indicated the leash at which he was tugging, and looking back, I saw the hesitant little setter following him reluctantly. That shows you the type of man he is. He was crawling out from under with a ten-dollar dog.

"We came, at last, to a bush-grown ditch, and beyond it lay a thousand acres of rolling stubble. It was quail country, and Tichnor kept it heavily stocked. It was a great course. Tichnor addressed the group. 'You are agreed on the rules, gentlemen? The first dog to make a productive point shall be declared the winner?'

"They agreed as one man.

" 'Then,' said Tichnor, '*let them go.*'

"We unsnapped our leashes and the dogs sailed over

the ditch and out across the stubble in as pretty a getaway as I ever saw. All but one. Tyler's Jack didn't show any burst of speed. He just nosed up to the edge of the ditch and stood there. We were watching the race, forgetting all else, when I heard someone shout, 'Point, Judge. Point.' It was Tyler. His dog stood at the edge of the wet ditch, pointing staunchly into it. Tyler said, 'Steady, Jack,' and went up to the dog. Then he laughed. 'It's a productive point, Judge. Look!'

"We gathered around. In the ditch, trying to hide in the shallow water, lay—what do you suppose?"

"I don't know," I confessed. "A hippopotamus?"

"A mud turtle," he said. "An insignificant little, striped mud turtle.

" 'Well, Judge,' said Tyler, grinning. 'I await your decision.'

"Tichnor looked across the stubble at the field of dogs. They were still going gloriously.

" 'It is a productive point,' he said. 'Gentlemen, I have no alternative. I declare Tyler's Jack the winner of this event.'

"I'll say one thing for the crowd. They took it without a whimper, although they were pretty quiet on the way back to the house. Tichnor took us inside and we did what we could to drown our sorrows.

"It was while we were in there that I heard a clock striking three. 'Three o'clock,' I said. 'Where has this day gone?' And then I remembered. Honestly, Bill, that was the first time today that the thing had entered my mind. You can imagine how I felt. I suppose I was in the car in less than ten seconds. When I got out on the macadam I opened it up. That's a sweet car, Bill. Ninety is just a road gait for it but I suppose I should have slowed down a trifle on that double curve. Something happened—I don't know what— but I stood on my head for miles and miles. I don't think we hit anything but an occasional tree and fence post but, honestly, Bill, it was minutes before we stopped. I got out and walked to the nearest house. It was a mile away. They didn't have a car, so I telephoned here. I'm done for, Bill. Swamped, ditched, busted. And through no fault of mine, either. That's what makes it so hellish hard. She will never understand that I was blameless. She—"

The door of the garage swung open and my mechanic came out with the tire.

"That tube was cut in three places," he said. "I put in a new one. Shoe's all right."

I heard him, but my mind was elsewhere. In the garage a radio was blaring the daily news of the county. My ears caught the words, "Nick Stewart." I listened.

"—rich young sportsman," the voice said, "who disappeared from his spacious estate sometime during the night or early morning. His bed was rumpled and the room presented a disorderly appearance, as though he had left it hurriedly or had been forced from it. Mr. Stewart was to have been married at high noon today, to Miss Alicia Wainwright, of New York City and Stewartville. Mr. Stewart's family are much disturbed over his disappearance, while his fiancée is prostrated with grief. It is feared that he has been abducted and is being held for ransom. The police have been notified and preparations are being made to comb the surrounding countryside for some trace of the missing young millionaire."

Nick groaned piteously. "I can never square it now," he said. "The police are after me. I'm sunk."

"You're saved," I told him. "There's your story, made to order for you. You have been kidnaped. You overcame your guard and escaped. Call it four guards—Heaven knows you look the part. Tell that story and stick to it, and don't, for the love of Saint Regis, mention dogs. Get in— on the other side. I'll drive."

THE WHITE ALLY

GLENN ANDERSON awoke abruptly. The sanctity of that sunny glade was being rudely disturbed. The rustling of bushes and the tread of heavy feet came steadily nearer. Some one, a human by the sound, was hurrying faster than is the custom of those who haunt the wooded trails.

Then his ear caught a new sound, a faint patter of light, fast flying feet, accompanied by the silvery tinkle of a small bell. The sound came into hearing with the swiftness of a cloud shadow moving over an open field and would have as swiftly vanished had not the heavy footsteps suddenly ceased and a shrill whistle burst, with startling intensity, on the quiet air. With equal suddenness the sound of the bell ceased.

"Count!"

Anderson started, involuntarily, at the harshness of the voice. Venom fairly oozed from the spoken word. He even felt himself tremble slightly as he sat up straighter and listened. He knew what the tinkle of that bell meant for this was grouse country. A bird dog, young probably and out of control, was going "on his own" somewhere in the cover.

Again the shrill whistle cut the silence. Two short blasts—the universal signal to "come in."

Anderson, listening, caught the hesitating, reluctant tinkle of the bell as its wearer advanced slowly toward the point from whence that whistle emanated.

"Come here." This time the voice was silkily smooth but even Anderson detected the malice in it. The silvery tinkle stopped abruptly and a muttered curse came from the direction of the hidden hunter. Again the whistle sounded and once more the bell announced that the dog was coming closer. Coming, Anderson surmised, in fear and trembling, knowing by previous experience what was in store for him.

At last he came into view and the silent watcher gasped in involuntary surprise. He had expected to see an animal of nondescript color, come shrinking, belly to earth to take a beating but in this he was mistaken.

It was a snow white setter that stepped from behind a bit of concealing evergreen and paused, momentarily, in a sunlit opening in a listening attitude. There was no groveling in that poise. The silky coat with just a suggestion of wave in it, the short tail held stiffly straight, the low hung ear and square muzzle proclaimed this to be a dog of royal ancestry—an aristocrat by birth.

Again came the tramp of heavy feet. The screen of alders and matted vines parted and a red faced, thick set man stepped into the opening. A hunting cap, pushed back from his forehead revealed an apelike slant to the frontal bone. His little eyes, half closed in anger, were set too closely together and every feature was convulsed with rage. In his left hand he carried a shotgun but his right hand grasped a heavy dog whip which he carried butt foremost.

Anderson got quickly to his feet although the effort caused him to cough raspingly. As the stranger turned he advanced smilingly.

"A very handsome dog you have there, neighbor, and an exceptionally intelligent one, too, I should judge. How old is he?"

"Old enough to know a d—n sight more than he does," the red faced one growled surlily. "Come here you."

Anderson chose to ignore the deliberate rudeness of the reply. "An intelligent animal," he said smoothly, "but a very easy one to spoil. Use him gently and he will make you a good dog."

"Who asked you for advice?" The red faced one's tone was vitriolic. "I gave two hundred dollars for this pup and a lot of d—n fool advice like yours and I've had about enough of both. He is going to be broken to hunt close in cover and he's going to be broken now. If you don't like the idea you can hit the trail; see?"

Anderson's lips set in a firm, straight line. "Let me tell you, sir, I will not permit you to beat that dog without registering a vigorous protest. A whipping, perhaps, if it would relieve your feelings, but no cruelty. That is final."

The red faced man deliberately removed his shooting coat which he tossed across a low bush, then turning he faced the lighter man belligerently, the dog whip still grasped in his hand.

"So you won't permit it, hey? You go home and eat a good beefsteak and then come back and I'll talk to you. Now I have to hold my breath for fear I'll blow you away. So you won't permit it, huh? Well, let's see."

He advanced to the dog, seized him by the collar, lifted him clear of the ground and brought the loaded butt of the whip down across his back with crushing force. As he raised it aloft for another blow a soft exclamation at his elbow caused him to turn his head. In all probability his eyesight was normal but he failed to see the perfectly timed right that landed fairly on the point of his jaw with all the skill and weight and just wrath that was Anderson's behind it.

Had it been a year earlier he would have been felled like an ox but Anderson was lighter by forty pounds now and his strength had deserted him.

As it was, the big man staggered and his knees gave a trifle but he recovered instantly. With a bellowing roar he dropped the dog and brought the loaded butt of the whip down on Anderson's head with all the brutal ferocity of his cave ancestors.

Without a sound Anderson dropped in a crumpled heap on the mossy carpet and, after a time, silence reigned once more—the murmuring silence of a deserted wood.

It was a long time before Anderson stirred. He had been conscious for some minutes, while memory struggled back, but the effort to move seemed too great an undertaking to attempt. Now, as he lay there quietly and tried to control the bewildering pain at the base of his brain, he became aware of a peculiar, sobbing noise, as of labored breathing, somewhere close by.

He tried to analyze the sound but his sluggish brain refused to struggle with the answer and, at last, he slowly turned his head.

The white setter lay beside him, with closed eyes and flecks of blood on his silky coat. He breathed with a peculiar, rasping sound that brought the man promptly to his feet although, a minute since, he would have called it a physical impossibility. A tiny rivulet murmured, lazily, a few yards away and to this he went. Stooping, an intense nausea seized him. He conquered it and returned to the dog with his hat filled with water. He let this trickle over the bruised head and body and, at last, the setter opened his eyes. Great brown eyes they were and the pathetic appeal in them brought Anderson to his knees beside the beautiful animal. He tried to pet him, to soothe the hurt of those hideous welts, but again that terrible dizziness assailed him and this time he pitched forward on his face and lay silent and still beside the wounded animal.

It was the soothing hurt of a rough tongue licking the ugly gash in his scalp that brought him back to the world of reality and he turned his head enough to see the dog sitting, rather shakily, beside him and rendering a vigorous first aid. From where he lay Anderson stretched out a shaking hand and patted the dog's head.

"Blood brothers!" The phrase seemed to please him and he repeated it. "Blood brothers, old timer. Is it worth the effort to try and get home or shall we lie here and let nature take its course?"

The dog whined and got stiffly to his feet and, with tightly pressed lips, Anderson did likewise.

"All right, old boy; we'll make a try for it. You follow me; I know the way."

What that effort cost them only the man and dog knew and they never told. Arrived at his boarding house Anderson retired to his room, taking the dog with him, and phoned for the doctor.

The medico's curiosity was pardonable but Anderson

vouchsafed him no information. "A little accident, Doctor, that is of no consequence other than that it brought me a new friend. Look him over first, please. He's in far worse shape than I."

"I may not rate very highly as a veterinary," the doctor said, "but I am inclined to disagree with you. The dog is battered and bruised, but a few days' rest will make him as well as ever. Your case, Parson, is different—vastly different. I am going to speak frankly to you. I have contemplated doing so for some days but have hesitated for reasons which you cannot, because of your condition, understand. Overwork, coupled with too much study and too little out of doors exercise, has broken your health, but it has done something infinitely more serious. In every man there is an inborn instinct of self-preservation, a subconscious but powerful will to live which is, in a larger sense, the one important factor of life itself."

Anderson laughed, a mirthless ejaculation that was not good to hear. "In my case, Doctor—"

"It is your case which I am specifically discussing," the doctor said. "That impulse to exist is a factor which is essential to life. In your case that impulse is atrophied. You have come to a stage where you can contemplate the cessation of life with no regret. I have told you you have no organic trouble. Your body is still fundamentally sound."

Anderson raised a thin white hand and contemplated it with a sardonic grin. "Indeed, yes, Doctor. As sound as a dollar. Look at that hand. You couldn't truthfully call that a mailed fist, now could you?"

"There is nothing more difficult than to convince a man against his will," the doctor answered. "I shall continue to speak plainly. If you go on as you are now you will be dead in less than a year. If you follow my advice, and adopt the correct mental attitude, I have every reason to believe you will regain your health. The decision rests with you alone, but I hope you will be amenable to reason. Give up everything and go somewhere for a good long rest. You have no restraining ties other than your church. Your duty to yourself comes before everything else."

Again that bitter laugh. "I owe nothing to myself. I owe little to the church—except, perhaps, an apology. I have said many things from the pulpit, the truth of which I have come to doubt of late. I am a traitor to the cloth."

"It is your mind which is the traitor. Listen, please. There's a little shooting lodge out in Oklahoma that belongs to me. It's just a shack, but it is a comfortable one and it is yours for as long a period as you care to use it. Take this dog and go out there for a few months. Live in the open and give nature a chance. Put up a real fight and you will live to thank me some day. Will you do it?"

"I suppose so, Doc," Anderson said, listlessly. "I am afraid the battle will be neither fierce nor long but, well— you're the doctor. I'll go."

A month later, on a day when the sapphire sun floated noon-high in an unclouded amethyst lake, Anderson came to the door of his little cabin and half climbed, half fell into the hammock swinging from the porch rafters. The snow white setter, asleep on the steps, arose as he opened the door and stood in an expectant attitude, his plumed tail waving a cordial greeting.

As the figure collapsed in the hammock, wracked by a spasm of coughing, the dog came forward and thrust his cold muzzle into the white hand that hung so limply over the hammock's edge and the soft, brown eyes glowed when, after a minute, that muzzle received a friendly little squeeze.

He turned then and stood at the top of the steps, looking wistfully at the panorama before him. The cabin stood at the top of a little knoll and in every direction the land fell away in long, rolling waves, until they merged into the hazy indistinctness that clothed the purple hills in the distance. The crest of every wave was a somber brown, for it had not rained in weeks, and the Oklahoma sun had long since drained them of their moisture but the hollows were still luxuriantly green and the flags and water grasses stood straight and tall.

Anderson, seeing the dog thus, spoke quietly. "Sorry, old fellow, but I don't feel up to it today. If you wish you may go alone, though."

The setter walked slowly down over the steps and then turned, hesitatingly. Anderson reassured him. "It's all right, old man. Go on."

There was a flash of white and the dog was gone. Anderson, turning laboriously in the hammock, saw him, a hundred yards away, skimming across the brown earth, running without effort but fast—inconceivably fast.

He was still going, bulletlike, a quarter mile away, when he slid to an abrupt stop, doubled like a flash of light, swung to the right at a sharp tangent, roaded a few feet and stopped—as rigid as a thing of marble.

Anderson reached for a pair of binoculars that hung on one of the porch pillars and focused them on the dog. They brought him into sharp relief and the man forgot himself, momentarily, in a glow of pride for here was an effect which many artists have striven to paint and which comparatively few have attained.

As immobile as a thing of bronze, there was yet plainly discernible, even at this distance, some intangible quality that made of the whole a vital, dynamic force.

Anderson was gazing enraptured when a horse and rider came abruptly into his field of vision; the horse moving at a brisk canter and the rider, a woman, riding easily, like one long accustomed to a saddle.

While yet a few yards from the dog she drew the horse to a halt and slid gently to the ground.

Lightly she advanced until she stood beside the white statue. Anderson, watching eagerly, fancied he could see her lips move. Then she stooped, gave the setter a brief petting on his silvery shoulder and stepped in front of him.

She had gone less than ten yards when, from the weeds ahead of her, there was a sudden eruption of a score of hurtling brown bodies and, even at that distance, the watcher caught a faint murmur of the roar of their wings.

Count had "nailed" in champion style a bevy of prairie chickens which had sought the coolness of the damp ground during the noonday heat.

For an hour, then, the invalid had a wonderful time. The rider had mounted and was following the white streak that, like a flash of light, was off after the scattered birds. With growing admiration he watched the dog's great, slashing casts in search of the quarry, saw him flash into point after point as, one after another, he picked up the singles and held, statuelike, until the rider had dismounted and flushed the bird.

It was over at last and the rider headed her mount up the long slope to the cabin and, though the pace was fast, the dog ran in easy circles about the galloping horse.

As they drew nearer, the man, conscious of the rudeness of his stare, lowered the glasses and sat up in the hammock but already the powerful lenses had assured him that the rider was young and strikingly attractive in an outdoor, athletic way. There was a golden glint in her hair but, as she drew still nearer, Anderson decided it was a rich, chestnut brown. Her skin was of that creamy type which alike defies the wind and sun and, as she drew rein at the steps, he noticed the graceful beauty of her bare hands.

He came to his feet with an effort that sent him into a fit of coughing and he was obliged to grasp a pillar for support. When it had passed he found her standing at his side.

"You should not have arisen on my account," she said and her voice was low and musical. "Let me get you a chair or help you back to the hammock. I did not know you were ill or I would—I was about to say I would not have disturbed you, but what I really meant was that I should have come sooner."

She brought a chair forward and, despite his protests, forced him into it. Then she seated herself on the railing, one booted foot swinging rhythmically, and looked down on him with compassionate eyes.

"Thanks," he said feebly, after a moment. "You are very kind. I feel that I am exceedingly rude to accept a chair and leave you to sit standing, but this is the only chair the little shack affords. Won't you sit in the hammock?"

"Really, I musn't stop. I should have been home now but I just *had* to watch your wonderful dog work. He is yours, I suppose? I saw him on the steps when I passed early this morning."

"Yes," Anderson admitted. "He is mine. Come up, Count."

Count came up the steps sedately, thrust his muzzle into the man's hand for the affectionate squeeze and dropped at his feet.

"He is a beauty," the girl said, "and as good as he is beautiful. I have never seen such speed and his nose is perfect. What is his breeding?"

"I don't know," Anderson replied. "I acquired him by accident, as it were. Yes, I am sure 'accident' is the correct word. I have no pedigree of him."

"He is the perfect Prince Rodney type. I should be very proud of him if he were mine."

"I will remember that," Anderson said soberly. "I am very anxious that he be placed in good hands after I am— after I have no further use for him. He has been unfortunate enough—poor fellow."

There was a quick gleam of sympathy in the girl's eyes and her voice had a hearty, reassuring ring in it as she said, "Oh, I am sure you will keep him as long as he lives. He is a very wonderful dog and, if I owned him, I would not part with him for any consideration."

Anderson smiled grimly. "Thanks for the thought which prompted the speech but I am no longer deceived as to my condition. I have been facing the naked truth for some days now. I am sure you would be very kind to Count and if you will bring writing materials from my table I will be glad to give you a bill of sale of him now. I have worried much concerning his ultimate fate."

"You talk as pessimistically as Dad does when I do not feed him properly." Then as a sudden thought struck her. "What did you have for breakfast? Come, 'fess up. What did you eat?"

"I wasn't hungry," Anderson told her with a smile. "My appetite and my health eloped together. I believe I didn't eat anything this morning."

The girl frowned. "And last night?"

"Oh, I opened a can of something then. Tomatoes, I think. Really, I have quantities of food."

"And who looks after you—does the work, I mean? Cooking, washing dishes and those things?"

"We don't believe in work, Count and I. We have

taken out cards with the I. W. W.'s What little cooking there is done I do. Count washes the dishes."

The girl slid from the railing and stood erect. "I must be going," she said. "I will see you again, soon. We are neighbors, you know. Dad owns a small ranch over by the river. It's only seven or eight miles. We shall expect you to visit us some day, you and Count. Well, good-bye." She flitted down over the steps, swung into the saddle and was gone.

"Not at all conventional," Anderson thought, "but good. The kind of girl one can rely on to do the unexpected thing at the unexpected moment and still be right. And I didn't even ask her name. Well—it doesn't matter."

Two hours later he was awakened from fitful slumber by the rataplan of galloping hoofs and opened his eyes to find the girl again dismounting before the steps. At the cantle of the saddle a large covered basket was lashed and, in one hand, she carried a huge milk can. She greeted him gaily.

"I thought I'd bring you a sample of our dairy products," she laughed. "If you like them perhaps you will consent to become a regular customer." She placed the can on the steps and proceeded to unlash the basket.

"These were eggs when I started," she chattered on before Anderson could speak. "Fresh eggs from our Wyandotte pens but quite likely they resemble an omelette now. Dixie didn't like the can hammering her side and traveled fast. There, aren't they beauties? And not one of them even cracked. Now, if you will forgive the liberty, I'll step inside and prove to you how naturally eggs and milk mingle in each other's society."

She was inside the cabin before he could do more than mutter inanely. Soon he heard the rattle of dishes and, presently, the staccato beat of a fork in an earthen bowl.

He sat up in the hammock and smoothed down his rumpled hair. There was something reminiscent in that metallic sound. A homelike feeling suddenly permeated the atmosphere and he recalled again those boyhood days when he had watched his mother preparing dinner in that little home back in the Vermont hills. He was lost in reverie when a soft voice at his side recalled him to himself.

"Will you kindly drink this sample," the voice said, "and give me your opinion concerning its merits?"

He looked up. The girl stood before him with a serving tray in her hands. He suspected it was the battered old relic he had inherited with the cabin but a linen napkin of snowy whiteness covered it completely. There was a spotlessly clean glass upon it and a pitcher filled to the brim with a creamy, yellow fluid that still effervesced from the vigorous stirring it had received.

Anderson had not known the pangs of hunger for weeks but now he suddenly felt his tongue growing moist. He reached eagerly for the glass and she filled it to the brim. He raised it to his lips and when he lowered it again it was empty.

"Thanks," he said. "That was wonderful. I haven't tasted anything in weeks—yes months—like it. You are very kind."

"Nonsense," she replied. "I am merely trying to gain a new customer." She filled the glass again and extended it but he declined it.

"It is excellent," he said, "but it has property which, in our boyhood days, we used to designate as 'filling.'"

"That is only one of its many merits," she told him, "but you must drink it all—yes, every drop. I shall not leave until you have finished it."

Anderson leaned comfortably back in the hammock. "That being the case, I shall take my time," he declared firmly. "One should never bolt one's food but each mouthful should be interspersed with conversation, preferably of a light nature. I read that in 'Diet and Health.' It sounds logical, doesn't it?"

"Quite. Let's be frivolous. What shall we discuss?"

"For a light topic we might talk about myself. I'm nearly fifty pounds lighter than I was a year ago."

"All the more reason for your finishing that eggnog. You'll be pounds heavier then."

"I'll try it presently. I feel, though, that under the circumstances I should introduce myself. We seem to have no mutual friends. My name is Anderson—Glenn Anderson. You'll have to accept me at my face value, which is a very poor recommendation, I fear."

"Not at all. It is the best of recommendations for it is so easily read. I am Jeanne Corliss."

"Honestly?" Anderson asked. "That merely goes to prove how stupid I am. I thought you must be Florence Nightingale."

"Oh, no." Her laugh was spontaneous and musical. "Not even one of her disciples. I am merely a saleswoman in search of a new customer. And now you must take another glass."

He drank it dutifully. "Is there much more?" he asked.

"Why? Are you so anxious for me to go?"

"Indeed no. I was wondering, instead, how long it would last."

"There are at least two glasses more and you may take your time about drinking them. I am in no hurry and Dad never worries about me. Tell me about yourself, please."

"Sorry," he said, "but that is a direct violation of Rule twenty-three, Chapter Six, of '*Health In The Open.*' Choose a pleasant topic for conversation, is the theme song of that rule. Another one advises, with equal directness, 'Do not talk about yourself!' You can readily see, if I follow these rules, I must think and talk only about you."

Double rows of gleaming white flashed, momentarily, as she smiled. "I think this will be interesting. According to your silly rules I can't think or talk about myself either, but if you expect me to remain dumb you will be disappointed. Shall we begin?"

Anderson regarded her gravely. "Your eyes have that same shade of brown which makes your hair so attractive. Quite an unusual—"

"How blue the sky is," she interrupted, "and how cloudless. We do need rain, though."

"Remarkably precocious, too, for one so young. Let me see. Seventeen, I think she was, on her last birthday."

"Nine and eight are seventeen—and three are twenty. Aren't mathematics fascinating?"

"Positively thrilling. And isn't the theory of relativity the cutest thing? I adore it."

They talked nonsense for a half hour and Anderson knew long minutes when he was lifted bodily from the depressing weight that dragged him down. But the old cynicism would creep in, despite his efforts to forget and, when Jeanne arose, at last to go, her eyes were bright with unshed tears. Her manner, though, was still light and frivolous as she went down the steps and swung lightly into the saddle of the waiting Dixie. Count, begging another workout, pranced around the horse in mute ecstasy.

"Some day, soon," she promised him, raised her hand to Anderson in a little gesture of farewell, and departed at a brisk lope. The white setter came back and curled up on the steps but his soft eyes watched the retreating figure which rode so easily it seemed almost a part of the horse. Anderson watched it likewise. When it disappeared beyond the distant rise, he sighed heavily, lay back in the hammock, and let a new bitterness engulf his soul.

The next morning he arose an hour earlier than usual and spent more than the customary period of time at his morning ablutions. When he opened the door and stepped out on the porch the sun was only an hour high and the valley mists were just dispersing in wispy streamers above the remote hills. There was a tingling freshness in the air unlike any he had ever experienced and, involuntarily, he threw back his shoulders.

"It's a beautiful morning, Count," he said to the setter who stood beside him. "We will take a little walk after— after you have had your breakfast."

But after the dog had eaten, he lingered. He tried to read but found it hard to focus his attention on the printed page. Unconsciously his eyes kept straying to the west where the winding border of trees that fringed the river could be dimly seen.

It was after nine o'clock when she came, as radiant as the morning. Anderson threw the book aside and arose to meet her. Her greeting was as cordial as though they had known each other for two years and, in a few minutes, he again heard the clatter of the fork in the kitchen as it whipped the eggs to a creamy froth. But when she brought out the tray and set it on his knees he met with a disappointment.

"If you don't mind I'd like to work Count while you are taking your breakfast. Father has some fine setters and runs them in all the field trials but I am obliged to confess that we have none of this fellow's caliber. May I take him?"

"Certainly." He did not fancy the idea but found some small consolation in the fact that she would be obliged to return. "The fellow that coined that phrase about 'leading a dog's life' was laboring under a delusion. I envy Count," he said.

She chose to misunderstand him. "Oh, I am sure that you will be running all over the country in a very few weeks," she said. "Come, Count."

Anderson watched them go, the girl, the horse and the dog; each aquiver with animate, pulsing life and when they were gone he sighed. Just a short time ago he had been like that—and now—

He was lost in reverie, the breakfast untasted, when they returned. He received a scolding for his neglect.

"I dislike eating alone," he protested in defence. "Please join me in a glass of this delectable home brew."

"I had mine before I came," she said, "and I never, never eat between meals. Then, too, this is yours. You must drink it all. It's what you need."

Dutifully he obeyed and when the pitcher was drained she carried it into the cabin and he heard her washing dishes at the sink. She returned shortly and shook an admonitory finger at him in mock seriousness.

"From now on," she told him, "you must drink that much at least four times a day—and oftener if you can. You haven't ordered it but I am going to supply you with the milk and eggs until you are able to come after them yourself. Is that satisfactory?"

"Eminently so. Produce your dotted line and I'll sign."

"And you will drink it four times a day? You promise?"

"I have, with a fervor which surpasses even yours, exhorted men not to drink—but I'll promise, certainly."

"Thanks," said Jeanne, gratefully. "And now that we have settled that let's talk about another thing. Why can't I enter Count in the State Trials, next week?"

"The State Trials?"

"Yes. The Oklahoma trials for bird dogs. Dad has four dogs entered but I'd like to take Count and show them what a real bird dog is supposed to do."

"What do you—I hope you'll pardon me—but what do you know about it, anyway?"

"What do I *know?* Or did you say what do *I* know about it? Either way it sounds like thinly veiled sarcasm but I'll answer it just the same. I have been with Dad every year since I can remember to almost every field trial of importance in the United States. I have learned *something* about it. I know it takes a good dog to win any of these events but I know Count does better work than any young dog I have ever seen. With proper training he can win the National Championship."

"Aim high, young man. Aim high."

"You don't believe it but I am telling you what I know. There is only one really great dog he would have to beat and that is Regorap. He won last year but they may not enter him again this season. He was sold recently and I don't know whether his new owner intends entering him or not."

"Oh, I hope they do. It would be all the more honor for you to win from the champion."

"You'll let me enter him then in the State Trials?" Her

face was all eager animation and she seemed more like a child than a young woman.

"Of course you may, if you wish. He is yours anyway—or will be soon."

Jeanne turned on him fiercely. "Don't ever, ever let me hear you say anything like that again. If I do you will be minus one perfectly good milkmaid."

The sun was just sinking over the western hills one afternoon a week later when Anderson, absorbed in a magazine, was brought to himself by the rattle of approaching wheels. He glanced up and saw Jeanne driving up in a spring buckboard, accompanied by a lean, wind-tanned, athletic man of middle age whom he instinctively judged to be her father. Count, spotlessly white as usual, sat proudly between them.

They halted at the steps and Anderson, with an alacrity which he had not displayed for weeks, arose to meet them, but Jeanne had jumped, even as the horse halted, and intercepted him. She seized his hand and shook it warmly.

"You are the owner of a field trial winner," she told him, happily. "Oh, it was wonderful, wasn't it, Dad? I beg your pardon—Dad, this is Mr. Anderson of whom I have told you so much. Mr. Anderson, my father."

Mr. Corliss had descended from the wagon and now

hastened forward to shake hands. "I have wanted very much to do this since I saw your dog put down yesterday morning," he said. "I have never seen a young dog of his caliber and I am not what one would call a novice at the game. When the judges gave the word he was off like an arrow—didn't even stop to look at his brace-mate. He was on the skyline every minute—as swift and as smooth as a swallow and yet he handled perfectly. And *staunch*—a pair of horses couldn't drag him off point. There's a great future ahead of him."

"I think he is a very nice dog," Anderson replied, "and I am deeply attached to him. We are what I have sometimes called blood brothers. There is a story connected with my manner of acquiring him that I feel you should know."

Jeanne clapped her hands ecstatically. "Oo-o! A mystery, Dad. I knew there was one. Do tell us. Please."

They found seats and Anderson told them of the manner in which he had acquired the dog. The story suffered much in the telling, for he touched but lightly on his own actions and subsequent injuries, but Corliss, watching him keenly, read between the lines.

"So you see," Anderson concluded, "I am without legal claim on the dog. Perhaps it would be better not to exploit him further. His former owner may turn up at any time and brand me as a thief."

Corliss stood up and threw back his muscular shoulders. "I hope he tries it sometime—when I am present. If there's any one thing I can't stand it's the abuse of dumb animals. And you have no idea who the man was?"

"Not the slightest. Those particular covers are almost nationally known. There is nothing in New England that surpasses them for grouse. People come from all parts of the country to work their dogs there and to shoot over them. This was no local man—of that I am sure."

"You have every moral right to claim ownership," Corliss said. "The contemptible brute! trying to force a dog that, for a score of generations, has been bred for speed, to work to a gun in the brush. It can be done but not by that method. The double-distilled, triple-plated fool!"

"Careful, Dad," Jeanne warned him. "Mr. Anderson is a clergyman, you know."

"Never mind that, Mr. Corliss," Anderson said smilingly. "I've thought of him often in worse terms than those and without the least bit of satisfaction, either."

"Well, at any rate," said Jeanne, "Count was entered in the trials in your name. Yes, and I took the liberty, after he won, of mailing an application and entrance fee for the Clayborne event to be held in Texas next week. That should give you some claim on him."

"I don't anticipate any trouble," Corliss assured him.

"The rotter left him for dead, there can be no doubt of that. The chances are a thousand to one he will never see the dog and, if he did, the odds would be almost equally great that he would not recognize him. If I were in your place I would enter him in every event throughout the circuit. He will pick up a nice bunch of money for you and a lot of honor for himself."

"I'll leave that to your daughter, Mr. Corliss. She is a far better manager than I."

Jeanne rewarded him with a glorious smile and danced down over the steps to the buckboard. From beneath the seat she extracted a paper wrapped bundle and, flitting back, placed it in Anderson's hands. "It's a little present to you from Count," she said.

It was a beautiful silver loving cup, properly inscribed and in its depths were five crisp twenty dollar bills.

"That is part of the purse," Jeanne explained. "The rest I spent on entrance and starting fees and carfare. I have it all figured out somewhere."

"Never mind trying to find it," Anderson urged. "You are president, vice-president, secretary and treasurer and also chairman of the board of directors. Just credit me with enough to settle my egg and milk bill and accept the remainder as a sort of contingent fund for operating expenses. In all probability he will not win again."

Jeanne gave him a long, direct look. "More than all else you need faith," she said.

Anderson began to gain a little of it when Jeanne returned the latter part of the next week with another silver trophy, a substantial sum of money and a tentative offer of a thousand dollars for the dog. She was highly elated. "Of course I told him Count was not for sale," she said, "but he persisted in making the offer. I do hope you will refuse it. I can win more than that with him this season and his value will steadily increase."

"They may as well understand first as last, that he is not, and I hope never will be, for sale," Anderson informed her, gravely. "Do you know I really would like to see him in competition and that is the first real ambition I have had in months."

Jeanne did a little quickstep of pure delight. "I am so glad," she cried. "I know you are better. Your face shows it and you are lots stronger than you were. Of course you shall see him work. Why, you'll be handling him yourself in a few weeks."

"Hardly that, I think, but I really do feel better and I have noticed for several mornings now that my belt refuses to fasten where it used to."

"And your clothes, too," said Jeanne. "At first they looked as though they were hanging on a nail but now they have begun to fit again. Now don't you think we have the best milk and eggs in the state?"

"Indeed I do," Anderson agreed. "You must have a very good business. How many customers have you?"

"Not many," Jeanne confessed. "You see, Dad planned on using most of our eggs and milk for the dogs. He has quite a large kennel—sometimes as many as fifty. I believe, yes, I am quite sure you are our oldest customer."

"And you have been making yourself all this trouble just out of the goodness of your heart? Oh, Jeanne—"

"It was nothing," she interrupted hastily. "We have more than enough, and, well, it is dog food anyway."

Anderson laughed, a genuine, wholehearted laugh. "Well, I am as hungry as a dog. Will you join me in a—dog biscuit or something?"

"I know what we'll do," said Jeanne. "I brought over some delicious comb honey—Dad opened a hive yesterday—and I'll make a pan of biscuits if you will permit me. Then we'll have lunch."

"Hot biscuits and honey," Anderson chanted. "Ambrosia and nectar. It's a meal fit for the gods. Will I permit it? I'll not only permit it but—I'll help."

It was on a beautiful December day some three months later that Jeanne, with her father and Anderson, stepped from the train as it halted at the little way station at Knox-ville, Tennessee, and hurried up to the baggage car to re-lease Count from his traveling crate. They were not the only travelers bent on a similar mission for Knoxville was the town nearest to that stretch of country which had been chosen for that greatest of all dog classics, the National Field Trials for bird dogs.

Anderson had been following the trials for several weeks but the novel character of the people he met was still a source of bewilderment to him. It had become a common occurrence to be introduced to some clear eyed, flannel shirted man who might well be a small local rancher, only to learn, later, that he was some well known financial genius. Likewise it was equally common to see the same financial genius linked arm in arm with another clear eyed, flannel shirted man who, in turn, proved to be a small local ranch owner. Gradually he came to know that these were cosmopolitan gatherings, drawn from far and near and made brothers by a common bond—the love of a good dog.

Rooms had been reserved for them at the little frame hotel and thither they went in a ramshackle taxi driven by a straw hatted boy of sixteen who knew bird dogs with a thoroughness that was surprising. They breakfasted sump-tuously for, despite its smallness, the cuisine of the hotel was excellent, and then sallied forth to procure mounts for the day. This done, they saw Count again carefully crated and headed for the starting point in a jolting and disreputable looking truck. They followed at a corresponding pace.

"As I figure it," said Corliss, "barring rotten luck which sometimes happens, there is no question but Count will meet the champion eventually and, if he does, it will be a battle I would not miss seeing for worlds. Aside from any personal interest I may have in the matter I hope he wins for two reasons."

"I am anxious to hear them, Mr. Corliss," said Anderson.

"Firstly, then, I favor the setter. As you know, the present champion is a pointer. I am sorry to say they have been winning the honors consistently for a number of years. Believe me sincere when I say I am not speaking disparagingly of the breed either, for they have won strictly on their merits, and the present holder of the title is, I believe, the greatest of them all. Giving them full credit for this, however, I am hoping to see the setter again come into his own for, of all dogs, I believe them to be the most lovable."

"I quite agree with you on that point. They seem to combine the affection and intelligence of the spaniel with the dignity and poise of the larger breeds."

"Exactly. In my opinion, no other breed possesses these qualities to such a degree. In the second place I am personally prejudiced against Boucher who owns the present champion. I have seen him but a few times but I dislike him immensely and am glad that I do for he is the type I cannot stand. Big, coarse, loud mouthed, a braggart and a bully and, worse than all else, newly and offensively rich. He bought the champion only a few months ago at a price which has not been disclosed but it must have been unprecedented or Moore, whom I count as a friend, would never have sold it to that brute. I believe he is the only owner of importance who is not what might be properly termed a gentleman."

"I hope it will not be necessary for us to meet him," said Anderson, "for, from your description, I should judge it might be an unpleasant episode."

"Oh, you'll meet him, all right, if Count gets into the finals. He'll be shaking a roll under your nose and daring you to cover it at any odds. That is his method."

Anderson laughed good naturedly. "Not if he learns of my financial standing. I am down nearly to the toe of my stocking."

"There is about eight hundred dollars of Count's winnings, you know," Jeanne interposed, "and you aren't a real minister—are you?"

"I never was, I am afraid. However, I should be opposed to betting it. But why worry?"

Corliss, however, would not dismiss the matter so easily. "He is about ripe for a killing," he said, "and I'd like to see him dry cleaned. There are a great many others who feel the same way and sometime the chance will come. When it does I want to be numbered among those present. Well, here we are and the first brace is out. Look at that fellow go, will you? That's Bowker's Flash. He's a good dog but lacks class."

In the drawing Count had been allotted ninth place and it was not until after the midday lunch that he was put down with his brace-mate. Anderson had long since become an enthusiastic fan and it was with mingled pride and excitement that he heard the judge read—"Will-o-the-wisp, by Jingo ex May Montrose, J. Purcell, owner, B. Reed, handler, with Count, pedigree unknown, G. Anderson, owner and Jeanne Corliss, handler. Let them *go*."

They were off at the word but Count so far outclassed the other dog that Anderson felt little interest in the event. He did, however, derive a quiet enjoyment in watching Jeanne, far ahead on horseback, directing the dog a quarter mile away, merely by the wave of an arm or some semaphorelike signal with the soft hat she wore and which she swung at arm's length when she wished to turn him. The large gallery, following at a respectful distance, were profligate in their praises.

So manifestly one-sided was the race that at the end of twenty minutes the judges ordered the dogs taken up and Anderson rode out to meet Jeanne, who was returning with Count running his customary circles about her. She was radiantly aglow and, as they met, she gave him a heart warming smile.

"Isn't he wonderful?" she cried. "All I have to do is just *think* what I want him to do and he does it. It's almost uncanny."

"He is a good dog," Anderson admitted, "but why give *him* all the credit? *I* shall not do so, at least. For a milkmaid you are the best handler I ever saw and I shall see that you receive credit for it."

"Nonsense. He doesn't need a handler. Just let him go and he will beat any dog in the world—except perhaps the champion, and I think, honestly, that he would beat *him*."

"That," said Anderson, "is something that only time can tell."

"A very short time," said Corliss. "He will be paired with the champion in less than a week."

That he was a true prophet was evidenced when one evening, some five days later, they went into the lobby to learn the judge's decisions for the day and the selections of the contenders for the morrow.

Their entrance created a stir and numerous people in

the gathering crowded forward to shake their hands. From the babel of conversation they gathered the fact that Count was slated to be put down with the champion the following day.

"What did I tell you?" Jeanne cried delightedly as she looked up into Anderson's face, a triumphant gleam in her brown eyes. "I knew they'd just *have* to do it. Isn't it splendid?"

Anderson was about to give her some light rejoinder when a blatant voice, close by, bellowed—"Where is this fellow, Anderson? Let me get to him and see how much he really thinks of his dog."

Jeanne, who was still looking up into Anderson's face, saw his lips twitch slightly and his dark blue eyes suddenly become steellike in their hardness as he turned to face the owner of the challenging voice.

He came, elbowing through the press, a big, red faced, coarse featured bulk of a man and he held in his uplifted hand a sheaf of banknotes that was awe inspiring.

But Anderson did not see them. For him the room had suddenly changed. Gone was the hushed throng of spectators and in their place was a little open glade in the Vermont woods and, in its center, a purple faced brute grasping a dog whip with the butt end foremost. Then the picture faded and he saw a setter lying on the ground, his body shuddering convulsively and his silky coat, that had been so white, rapidly growing crimson.

He came to himself with a start and gazed into the leering face so close to his own. He spoke quietly.

"I am the man you are looking for," he said.

Boucher, for this was he, thrust the sheaf of banknotes into Anderson's face. "Ten thousand at two to one that my dog wins."

"No, thank you."

"Afraid, huh?" Boucher roared. "Well, three to one, then?"

"No."

"Four to one?"

"No."

"Yellow," said Boucher. "I thought so. What odds do you want?"

"I am not looking for bets," Anderson informed him, "but if I were, I should look elsewhere."

"What do you mean by that?" Boucher roared.

Anderson gave him a mirthless little smile. "You may draw your own conclusions," he said.

Boucher's naturally red face went purple and his eyes bulged glassily as he struggled to speak, but Corliss pushed himself between them and grasped the angry man by the lapel of his coat.

"I don't share my friend's compunctions," he said shortly. "I'll cover that little roll of yours at even money. Pick your stake holder."

As if it were a signal Anderson saw a score of men surge forward, reaching for their wallets as they came, and close about the angry gambler. In the confusion he laid his hand on Jeanne's arm and drew her out on the veranda.

"That was he," he told her. "The brute who beat Count so cruelly. What shall we do now?"

Jeanne thought a moment. "He didn't recognize you. In all probability he will fail to recognize Count. I don't know what the outcome will be but I think we should play the game through."

"Right," said Anderson. "Win or lose, we'll play the game."

The judge spoke dramatically for he, as well as the greatly augmented gallery, knew that this was a great moment. History would be made in the next hour and he realized the responsibility he shared with his colleagues.

"Ladies and gentlemen. The next brace is Regorap, by Jingo ex Monica, C. Boucher owner, R. White handler—with Count, pedigree unknown, G. Anderson owner, Jeanne Corliss, handler. May the best dog win. *Let them go!*"

That this was to be a battle of champions was evidenced from the first moment. Count was as fast as the wind but, in that first wild dash so dear to the hearts of field-trial men, the lean pointer held him neck and neck and the position remained unchanged until they made a cast at slightly diverging angles.

For a half hour the battle raged and honors were even on the number of finds. Then Jeanne, firm in the belief that Count possessed the superior nose, changed her tactics and sent her dog cutting the path of the great pointer who had just gone, meteor-like, around the end of a weed patch. As the white setter, going equally fast, neared the patch he slid to a skidding stop, swung sharply about and pointed into the weeds.

"Point, judge," Jeanne called and, riding ahead of the dog flushed a large bevy. Corliss pounded Anderson on the back with his riding crop and shouted excitedly. "One more trick like that and the game is won. What do you think of that girl of mine? Brains—what?"

"Some day," Anderson answered smilingly, "I hope to tell you just what I think of her. She is—*look!*"

Again the setter had duplicated the previous find and again birds arose as Jeanne rode in front of the dog.

"That settles it," Corliss shouted. "That's his one weakness. He's game and fast and stylish and all that but

he hasn't Count's nose. They'll order them up now. Let's go on."

They rode slowly ahead to meet Jeanne who, at a signal from the judges, had brought Count in to heel. Together they rode toward the judges who were holding a brief consultation. As they neared them there came a sudden clatter of hoofs and Boucher thundered past and drew up beside the judges.

Anderson reined in his horse and spoke quietly to Corliss. "I have a suspicion that what he is about to say to them involves me. Will you escort your daughter to some other locality. Something unpleasant might happen."

"Indeed?" said Jeanne. "I'd like to see Dad, or anyone else, keep me away. I shall go with you."

Corliss squared his shoulders determinedly. "Jeanne is right," he said. "If it concerns you, we are interested. Let's go up."

They rode forward. Boucher, almost apoplectic in his fury, was shaking a paper before the judges and shouting vehemently. As they rode nearer the angry voice became distinctly audible.

"There's the certificate of registration," he was roaring. "You can't doubt that. He is my dog—I lost him six months ago. I wasn't sure at first but now I *know*. That d—n thief stole him from me. I'll have his hide, d—n him!"

One of the judges raised a remonstrating hand. "If you have any claim make it to the association," he said. "This is a field trial and not a court of justice. There's Anderson now. Settle the matter with him or with the local authorities."

Boucher turned and, seeing the approaching trio, came forward belligerently and reined his mount in at Anderson's side.

"I know you now, d—n you. Your face looked familiar last night but I couldn't place it. What kind of a thieving game are you trying to play, anyway? Think I ain't smart enough to know my own dog, you dirty crook?"

Before Anderson could reply Corliss cut in. "This is not your dog, Boucher. You relinquished every—"

"You're a liar," the bully yelled insanely.

Corliss smiled, a peculiar thin lipped smile. "And you," he retorted easily, "are a gentleman—which is the biggest lie I ever told. Get off your horse for a minute please. I have a keen desire to take you apart and see how you are made."

"I'm not talking to you," Boucher thundered. "I'm—"

"But I'm talking to you," Corliss interposed. "There's a little matter of ten thousand dollars of your money in the hotel safe waiting for me. Give me ten minutes of your time, somewhere alone, and I'll call the bet off."

"You go to h—l." He was almost incoherent now. "I'll

talk to you later." He turned on Anderson. "You're the dirty crook I want to get my hands on."

Anderson met his gaze steadily. "I'll not keep you waiting," he said evenly. "There's a clump of trees over yonder that will afford us seclusion. We may as well settle accounts now for some of them are long overdue."

He turned to Jeanne and looked into her eyes. They were grave and unsmiling but he fancied there was a look of quiet trust in them and the thought pleased him.

He lifted his cap. "Will you excuse me for a few minutes?" he asked. "There is a little matter that seems to demand my attention."

Then he received his smile—a full lipped, tender smile that breathed more of her supreme confidence and trust than any words could have done.

"Certainly," she said.

He bowed and turned to the storming Boucher. "Ready?" he said. "Well, let's go."

Boucher, like all bullies, was a coward when the odds of battle were equal, but here he felt they were to his liking. He outweighed his opponent by fifty pounds and, from past experience, he believed Anderson incapable of striking a dangerous blow. He would overwhelm him by brute strength, crush him to earth with a few powerful blows. Then he would take on Corliss and treat him likewise.

They had reached the sheltering trees and Anderson slid from his mount and removed his coat. Boucher, cursing venomously, followed suit and they stood facing each other on the smooth greensward with the trees protecting them from the sun's rays.

A similar setting, Anderson thought, to the other where he and the foul mouthed brute had met for the first act of their little drama. A similar setting, yes, but he fancied this act would have a different ending.

With a snarl Boucher rushed but Anderson side-stepped easily, delivering a smashing left as he did so. Boucher turned in an endeavor to clinch his opponent and bear him to the ground by his superior weight but the lighter man danced away from the clutching fingers and, as he retreated, he struck, again and again, shrewd, stinging blows that took toll, in some measure, for that other day when Count's white coat was stained a sickening red.

Failing in his attack, Boucher resorted to a frantic assault of pile driving blows and snarled in fiendish glee when he saw his adversary retreating before him.

Then, suddenly, in that careful retreat, Anderson stopped, lightly poised, his left foot advanced slightly and, in that instant, he struck with every ounce of his weight behind the blow. The timing was perfect and the blow landed as he had intended, full on the point of the jaw.

There could be but one possible result, for the blow would have felled an ox. Boucher stopped abruptly, his heels seemed to lift slightly from the ground and he struck heavily on his head and shoulders.

Anderson picked up his coat and slipped it on and, as he did so, was suddenly aware of a vigorous burst of applause. He looked up and saw, for the first time, that Corliss, Jeanne, the three judges and the majority of the gallery were drawn up in an appreciative semicircle about them.

He paid them no attention but stooped over his fallen adversary. He had regained consciousness and was struggling to sit up. Anderson assisted him in the process. When he had recovered his faculties sufficiently Anderson addressed him in a voice modulated to a pitch incapable of reaching the ears of the audience.

"What did you pay for Count?" he asked.

"An even two hundred dollars."

"All right. I'll pay you that amount and you sign the transfer of ownership on the back of his registration papers in your pocket and give them to me."

"Not by a d—n sight. I'll see you in jail for this."

"Listen to me, Boucher." Anderson's voice was level, dangerously so. "I thought this matter through last night. Either do as I have suggested or accept the alternative."

"And that?"

"I will personally report your case to the president of the S.P.C.A. In addition to that I will have you arrested on a charge of assault with a dangerous weapon, with intent to kill, and I'll have every dog man in the country to back me up with an unlimited amount of funds."

Boucher thought a minute.

"Give me your pen. I'll sign."

The sun was just setting behind the purple hills when Anderson, bathed and freshly clothed, stepped out on the veranda of the little hotel. As he did so Jeanne, who had been curled in a chair for the past ten minutes, arose and advanced with outstretched hands to meet him.

He folded them in both his own and Jeanne, looking down at them, noticed that, although they were lean and brown and hard, they trembled. Some woman's intuition, however, told her it was not from weakness.

For a long time neither spoke but each thrilled with the message they read in the other's eyes.

Then Anderson lifted his head and gazed in awed silence at the fading sunset. Low down on the horizon the soft crescent of a new moon gleamed silverlike and, in its fading, night was born. Soft, languorous, lovely night—with its sure promise of a beautiful morrow.

LADDIE

THERE were forty rounds in the ladder, spaced one foot apart and the ladder stood almost perpendicular. Forty feet to the little platform at the top. To Laddie, halfway up, the remaining distance seemed an unsurmountable object. Never before, in his two years of dog life, had the climb been so hard. He paused for breath and, looking down at the trainer below, whined softly.

He wished that he might remain there indefinitely but a quick, upflung hand from the trainer forced him to again resume the weary climb. Obedience to the master's every gesture was all that Laddie knew.

Round by round, foot by foot upward, until he stood at last on the little platform so close to the stuccoed ceiling of the Opera House that there was barely room for him to stand erect.

From far, far below came the voice of the trainer in his stereotyped speech—"Ladies and Jantlemun, I present to you—Laddie—in his death defying leap—" the words trailed off into an indistinct nothingness to Laddie as he bowed—to the right—to the left. That awful roaring when he—lowered his head—like that—

He looked downward to the floor below. Something

was radically wrong. The other dogs, sitting erect on their little pedestals, were grotesque travesties; blurred, indistinct figures which writhed and twisted in and out of his vision and would not remain stationary a moment.

Today the distance to the floor was appalling. That baffling, blue-white fog which swirled and eddied beneath him added to, rather than diminished the distance. Again Laddie whined as he did in his puppy days when he first looked down from a table edge to the floor.

Out of a vast void beneath drifted a voice, *the* voice: "Laddie will leap—life net—in my hands."

Always before, Laddie had enjoyed a pleasurable thrill at this moment. He did not understand the tense hush of the audience which always attended this instant just before the leap. The applause which invariably followed meant nothing to him but he was going back to his master by the shortest possible route and he knew there would be a word of praise from him when he scrambled out of the little life net. This was the greatest reward Laddie could imagine.

But this afternoon the whole world had changed. He was in the midst of infinite space. He had been seized upon by the unknown and, as countless other dogs have done throughout countless ages, he lifted his head and howled— the long drawn, wolf howl—a prayer—a supplication to that unknown.

Then Laddie thought; "Below—somewhere below—
was the master. If he could—reach him—why, everything—"

Laddie tensed his muscles and leaped. Always before,
these muscles had propelled him in a beautiful, arching
curve, outward and downward, far across the stage. But
today—

He did not hear the quick gasp from the audience, nor
see the frenzied leap of the master. He knew only one moment of dizzy flight through limitless space and then a dull,
heavy blow that crushed as with a mighty weight—and—
darkness.

When Laddie recovered consciousness he did not know
that the master had worked over him for hours. He did not
know that, in addition to the bruises he had received in his
fall, he was also suffering from dog distemper in its most
acute form. He knew only that the slight fever which, for
the past few days, had caused him to seek the coolest corners had now become a raging, seething flame which
burned out his very life and, true to the nature of all dogs
since the beginning of time, he longed to crawl away in
search of that cooling stream which flowed always just a
little distance ahead. To crawl on—and on—until the end.

Then, by some magic which he could not comprehend

the cooling stream was there before him, so close that he had but to lift his head and drink.

So feverishly intent was he that he did not hear the Boy when he entered and, after drinking his fill, he relapsed so quickly into his former comatose condition that he did not hear the conversation which followed.

" 's that the dog 'at got hurt?" asked the Boy.

"Yes," responded the trainer with a "how-in-thunder-did-you-get-in-here?" look.

"Did it hurt him much?" the Boy queried, not noticing the look.

The trainer was human and he was in trouble. The Boy was interested and the trainer opened his heart.

"He's battered and bruised and busted up some inside, I guess, but that ain't the worst of it," he said. "He was just the same as a dead dog before this happened. He's got distemper and I never noticed it until after he made the jump today. I don't know whether to take him on with the show or not. We've got to move after the act tonight and if I take him I'll have to keep him from the other dogs or they'll catch it. Oh Thunder! I suppose I might just as well put him out of his misery and be done with it but, take it from me, Kid, I hate to do it. He was one nice little dog—one darn nice little dog."

"Don't kill him, Mister," the Boy entreated. "What-

cher want to kill him for if he's going to die anyway? Gee! I wouldn't kill him if he was mine." Then, with just a hint of longing, "I ain't never had—a dog."

The trainer pondered a moment. "If I give you this one and he dies will you bury him in a nice, deep grave?"

The Boy was eight years old. Distance and depth meant nothing to him. "I'd—I'd bury him 'leven feet deep," he said.

Again the trainer was thoughtful. "I'll tell you what I'll do, sonny," he stated at last. "I'll see how he is after the show tonight and if I don't think he'll—that is, if I decide to give him to you I'll leave him here and you can come and get him in the morning, the *first thing* in the morning and —and you take good care of him, sonny, won't you?"

"Gee, Mister! you bet I will," said the Boy. "I'll be here at most four o'clock after him," and he went out, whistling.

After the performance that night, which, by the way, was disappointing because there was no "big jump" as advertised, the trainer gave Laddie a hurried inspection. "You don't stand more'n one chance in a thousand, old chap," he said gloomily, "but I'm going to take you along with the show. Can't never tell what might happen." Then he sought one of the attendants. "Put the dogs in their crates and have an expressman get them to the station in time for the eleven-forty west bound," he commanded.

The attendant was not very drunk. Certainly he was not enough so to see double but it is possible that he might have counted eighteen dogs where there were but seventeen. Or perhaps it was Laddie's fault. Always before this he had been the first to hear the attendant's whistle but tonight no sound reached his ears. How could it when he was so far away, pursuing that elusive water that rippled over the stones, so cool, so deliciously cool—just a few steps—farther on.

Laddie was not with the other dogs when the attendant opened the crates the next morning two hundred miles from the last stand. And be it said to the credit of the trainer that the attendant did not lose his job when, flustered and apologetic, he reported that Laddie had been left behind. He expected to lose it; he felt that he deserved to lose it, consequently he was surprised when he heard his employer tell him that "perhaps it was just as well." But he did not understand what the trainer meant when, after a long minute's thought, he muttered, "'leven feet deep."

But before this, Laddie had undergone a rough journey. It was "most six o'clock," rather than "most four o'clock," but even then the janitor grumbled that it was a "divvil of an earruly hour for a man to open up the Op'ry House so that a boy could get his dog."

Laddie remembered but little of that journey and but

little of the days immediately following. Faint memories there were of one long, long night when the sun forgot to shine for interminable hours; a night that was lightened, however, by a voice, a cheerful little voice and by frequent doses of something that choked him as he swallowed it and which he always fought weakly against taking but which, somehow, always gave him strength to live—just a little while longer.

Came a day at last when the sun arose once more, behind a gray fog bank to be sure, but still it was light and objects, large objects, could be seen quite clearly. Also the terrible thirst was gone which argued that the fever had passed and, although too weak to walk, Laddie was quite content to lie behind a kitchen range, a luxury he had never before known, and eat and sleep and thump his tail languidly when the Boy petted him.

Then the inevitable happened. Laddie had always known a master since he first opened his puppy eyes to the world and he had liked this master as much as he had been permitted but there had always been seventeen other dogs to share his affection—and Laddie was not a dog who could be satisfied with an eighteenth part.

Now, all at once he came to know real dog love. At first he could only lie with his head cocked a little to one side as he listened for the Boy's step, but in a few days he was able to walk again and, from that time on, he made it the rule of his life never, for one moment, when he could possibly prevent it, to let this new love god out of his sight.

When one has climbed through infinite space where chaos reigns supreme—and fallen then to the very uttermost depths into a lake of molten fire—only to be rescued at last by a love god, one should cherish that god above all things else.

So Laddie grew strong again, grew stronger in love: learned, too, what hate was, for he bitterly detested the fate that kept the Boy in the big red building six hours a day and five days out of every seven. He quickly learned to know the hour when the boys were permitted to come forth from the building for the last time that day and a few minutes before that hour he would be waiting just at the bottom of the steps, head again cocked a little to one side the better to hear the faint tap of the bell which always miraculously preceded the opening of the doors.

Then there was the other big building, where the love god went sometimes of an evening, and here, too, Laddie learned to wait outside, although he did not learn until he had several times been forcibly ejected by an usher—very forcibly once when he had stolen in in search of his love god and had barked fierce defiance at an elephant that walked boldly out of a white screen on the stage and was apparently bent on annihilating that god. But, although the usher hurried to reach him, Laddie yet had time to see the huge animal turn at the last moment and vanish into the nothingness from whence he came, and never for a moment did he doubt that it was anything but the fierce fury of his bark that caused the elephant to flee.

Laddie worried very much when the Boy was in this building. He did not consciously reason but instinctively he knew that danger lurked within. Had he not been whirled into space while in one of these buildings and suffered untold agonies as a consequence? When Laddie thought of this he sat up very straight and cocked his head a little more sharply to one side, lifting one ear a trifle the better to hear the first sound that told him his god was in danger and, be it said to Laddie's credit, although at every burst of applause from the audience the hair involuntarily bristled along his back, the only fear he knew was the fear that some harm was befalling the Boy. Laddie would have fought anything in the heavens above or the earth beneath had it attacked his divinity.

But, although he feared the place, there was a strange fascination about the Opera House for him. In his other life he had known no other world than these big buildings and, though now he was perfectly happy, yet there was a lingering memory of the old life, of the glorious frolics—and the glorious fights—with those other dogs which Laddie would be a long time forgetting.

Then came a day when he learned what real worry meant. He had hurried with the love god and several other boys to an old barn on the outside of which a man was pasting large sheets of colored paper. The boys were gleeful and Laddie frisked happily about and, in his exuberance, chased an inquisitive cat into the nearest tree and lingered to bark derisively at her for a few minutes.

Then, when he found she did not mind his ridicule, he left her and went back to the barn.

Instantly he knew something had happened. His god had changed. He was no longer a happy, laughing deity but, instead, a very serious, worried little boy. Shortly, too, he left the other boys and hurried homeward and although Laddie tried to entice him to play, as was their custom, he met with no success and soon gave up the attempt and walked quietly at the Boy's side, trying to make out what his mumbled monologue meant.

"The 'Mperial Dog Show, Friday night, in the Opera House," the Boy muttered. "They're comin' back here. I betcha he's heard that Laddie didn't die. I betcha he'll come after him but, by gosh, he won't get him. I'll hide him up in the shed and if he tries to get him I'll hit him over the head with a—a club or somethin'. I'll—"

The Boy was neither careful nor conservative in the use of his pronouns but he was very much in earnest—and the hair bristled a bit along Laddie's spine.

Followed three days of agony for both the Boy and dog. Neither ate well. The Boy ate through force of habit, the dog merely as a matter of necessity. And while the Boy fretfully slept, the dog lay with both eyes open, head up, listening—for something—he knew not what.

Friday night. To Laddie the air was pregnant with that intangible dread. The Boy was dressing to go out and his father was talking to him. Laddie sat in the middle of the room, listening.

"You had better put the dog up in the shed chamber," the Boy's father said. "He was a show dog you know, and a dog never forgets. He will follow you to the Opera House if you don't lock him up and he might run away with the show. I expect he misses the old life—don't you Laddie Boy?"

Laddie liked the Boy's father but he did not like the words "shed chamber." He knew what that meant. On several occasions, when it had not been deemed expedient for him to follow, he had heard these words and he knew that "shed chamber" meant weary hours of solitary confinement in that room at the head of the back stairs.

But when the Boy called him he followed, dejectedly,

head down, and even the fierce hug he received, just before the door closed, failed to restore his spirits. He knew that tragedy hovered in the foreground.

But poor, downhearted, little dog that he was, his condition of mind was far happier than that of the boy who walked with downcast eyes and shuffling feet, toward the Opera House.

The Boy had never entertained a doubt but that the trainer had given him the dog in good faith but, in his heart, he knew that the man had expected Laddie to die. What would happen if, by some mischance, the trainer should learn that the dog was alive and well again? Would he come and claim him for his own?

Had the Boy been a few years older he would have worried less. Laddie would have been securely locked in the shed chamber while the show was in town and he himself would have kept out of sight but, at the age of nine, discretion is sadly lacking, so he took the manly course and went to learn his fate.

He derived a little comfort, however, from the fact that they could not get his dog tonight without his knowledge and, when he had found a seat far removed from the boys' row in front, he sat stolidly waiting for the show to begin.

Less comfortably would he have sat could he have glanced for a moment at the sidewalk below. Very near the entrance of the building, with his head tipped a bit in a listening attitude and a drop of blood falling now and then from a jagged cut in his shoulder, where he had jumped through a window pane to the ground below, sat Laddie.

Several times as the door opened to admit late comers he tried to enter unobserved but always the man in uniform was there and, downheartedly, he finally settled himself to the policy of watchful waiting and, as the minutes dragged by and he sat there alone in the quiet, a change gradually came over him.

A year is a long time for a dog to remember but tonight Laddie thought of the old life. There was something reminiscent in the atmosphere and once, in the absolute stillness, he thought for a moment he had heard an old command in a voice he had long since forgotten.

Then the door opened slowly and a woman, with a sleeping child in her arms, came out. Laddie was interested in neither the woman or the child but he was interested in the door and when it closed he was on the inside. Up one flight of stairs he went, nosed open the swinging doors— and the old life was there before his eyes.

Dogs everywhere on their little pedestals about the stage, sitting erect and bright eyed, but what immediately attracted Laddie's attention was a little, brown haired, frightened dog halfway up a tall ladder.

Even as he looked came that well remembered, up-flung hand and the little dog tremblingly climbed another round—and stopped. Laddie trembled, too, and waited for the word he knew would surely follow.

"UP!" sharply, but before the little dog could obey came a mad scramble of feet down the aisle, a long, clean leap upward to the stage and Laddie was on the ladder. Before the other dog had climbed two rounds Laddie had reached him, had scrambled half over and half around him and in another moment stood on the little platform at the top; paused only to bow—to the right—to the left—and leaped in one beautiful, rainbow curve far out across the stage and landed lightly in the net which the trainer dazedly extended.

Instantly a mighty sound burst from the audience and the trainer seized the opportunity to fondle Laddie bewilderedly.

"Hello old boy! Where in the world—? I thought you was dead. And you came back, eh? Good old fellow."

He straightened up and came down to the footlights. "Ladies and Jantlemun—" He held up his hand for silence. "I—I don't know what to say. I—ah—I left this dog for dead when we were here—ah—when we last played before this well remembered audience and—er—er—"

It was not emotion so much as it was the inconvenience

of departing from his cataloged speeches which caused him to stammer but it gave the Boy his opportunity. He was already down to the very edge of the stage, and, in the momentary silence, he spoke, a clear, shrill treble that carried through the entire building.

"That's my dog, mister, and you—you just hand him right straight over."

Strange to say, no laughter followed this remark but rather a strained silence. Only the trainer smiled.

"Oh, no he isn't, Sonny," he said patronizingly. "I just asked you to bury him if he died, that's all. I'm much obliged to you for looking out for him."

The Boy fought back the tears which threatened to choke him. "You said if you left him I could have him, and you left him—and he's my dog."

The trainer was in a predicament. He did not wish to belittle himself before the audience but this dog was a valuable piece of property to him and he did not wish to lose it. He knew dogs and saw a way out of his difficulty.

Crossing the stage, he lifted a dog from his pedestal and placed the little seat in the center of the stage. A slight motion of his hand and Laddie was sitting erect upon it.

"Now I'll tell you what I'll do, Sonny," the trainer said. "If you can call this dog to you he's yours. If he wants to stay with me he's mine. That's fair enough, ain't it?"

"I don't have to call him; he'll—he'll follow me—anywhere," the Boy bravely answered but, as he turned and walked toward the door, he knew that this was merely empty bravado. He was playing a losing game. Laddie had come back to his own and he would never, never, see him again. Then the first bit of real manhood asserted itself in the boy. "If Laddie was happier—he didn't want to keep Laddie if Laddie didn't want to stay."

He was outside the swinging doors now and, all at once he was a boy again, a very little boy, and sobbing as though his heart would break, he ran down over the stairs—homeward.

So hard he sobbed that he did not hear the sudden thunder of applause that burst and beat through the empty corridors as a wave breaks upon a rock bound shore. He pushed the outer door open and hurried, still sobbing, down the street.

Then suddenly the Boy was laughing hysterically—for 'round and 'round him in swift, dizzying circles, barking madly the while, there leaped a little black and white dog.

THOROUGHBRED

THE little old clock on the mantel clicked warningly and then, after a moment, struck five tinny notes.

Old George stirred, rolled partly over, and one of his thin, blue-veined hands drew the faded coverlet a little closer about his shoulders. It was a cool morning for early September, and, when the fires of youth have fled, the blood chills easily.

It was hardly time, yet, to get up. It was not yet quite light. With eyes still closed Old George knew just how the room looked. The low posted walls with the faded yellow wall paper; the patch in the ceiling plaster that was such a perfect map of Texas. The long, winding crack that was the Rio Grande. Presently the sun would come up, and the light deflected from the faded curtains would illumine the framed photograph of Mary, and the grimy old lithograph of Custer's last stand.

In another half hour it would be light enough to see through the open doorway into the kitchen. How black and shiny the warped old stove always looked in the first light of dawn. Old George loved to polish things that would take a luster; the old copper above the kitchen sink—the brass door knobs—Tommy's silken coat.

When the clock struck six Tommy would begin to paw and whinny for his breakfast and a drink of water. Tommy was wise. In his fifteen years of life he had learned many things and had come to know that love was the greatest of them all.

Old George thought about Tommy now, and of Tommy's mother, Bess. He had ridden Bess—no, it wasn't Bess; it was her mother, Baby, he had ridden back from the Panhandle, over the old Santa Fé trail, to Maine. They had said a man got only one horse like her in a lifetime, but he had had three. Baby, then Bess, and now Tommy.

He remembered the morning Tommy was foaled. He had gone to the foot of the stairs and called, "Hey, Bud!" and Bud had growled in early morning surliness, "Oh, gosh! What is it?"

Bud had been pleased, though. At birth Tommy had that same shiny, dark chestnut coat with the white blaze in his face and the four white stockings.

"He's yours, Bud," Old George had said. "I want you to train him for yourself and make a partner of him. He's a thoroughbred, son." And Bud had said, "I haven't got time, Dad. I'm going west in the spring."

He remembered, too, how Mary had cried when he said it. Cried and clung to Bud and said, "But you're all we have, Bud. Don't go."

He remembered how he had put his arms about her shoulders and patted her and told her it was all right. "It is just what I did when I was his age, Mary," he had said.

"But *you* came back," she sobbed.

"He will, too, Mother," he had assured her. "You'll come back, won't you, Bud?"

"Of course," Bud had said.

He hadn't though.

At first he had written often. Once a week. Sometimes twice. But as the years went by the letters became fewer. Then one of Mary's came back unclaimed. She had waited as long as she could and then, one night—

Old George thought now of the look on the doctor's face, and the ruggedly sympathetic grip of his hand. The rest was confused, somehow. The flowers—the whispering —Mary asleep in the front room.

"Clang!" Half-past five. Old George drew the back of a thumb across his eyes and crept from his bed. He shivered slightly as he dressed, and his bent fingers fumbled with the buttons. He felt warmer, however, after he had hobbled out into the kitchen. The stove looked just great this morning. That Double X was the best polish he had ever used. He took off the front covers, dumped in a panful of chips and lighted them. He remembered that the wood was almost gone. He would have to see about that tomorrow.

The shiny copper tea kettle he drained in the kitchen sink and hooked the handle over the spout of the iron pump. He liked to pump that first kettle of water in the morning. At about the fifth stroke he would hear Tommy getting up out in the stable. That accomplishment was almost effortless with Tommy. He could do it with practically one motion. There he was now. Just "thur-rump" and he was up.

"Hey there," Old George called. "You be quiet now, doggone ya, or I'll come out there and tan your hide," and Tommy nickered softly and pawed his stall floor.

The chips were burning brightly now, so he put a few small sticks on them, closed the drafts and put the tea kettle on to heat.

Slipping on a faded brown sweater he opened the kitchen door and hobbled painfully out through the shed to the stable. "Hi there, you good for nothing old burro," he called as he opened the stable door.

Tommy's head was already thrust through the little window of his roomy box stall. His dark chestnut coat and flaxen mane proclaimed him to the world a thing of beauty, while the wide flaring nostrils, the little outstanding veins on his cheeks and the widely spaced, soft-hued eyes, bore mute evidence of his lineage. Tommy's blood was of the bluest.

There were not many oats in the barrel. When Old George had measured out Tommy's four quarts there were scarcely as many left.

He would have to see about that today. It wasn't so easy to ask, now that Lem was not a selectman. When Lem had been chairman of the board he had always said, "Sure, I'll write you an order, George. We've got to keep Tommy fed. How's the groceries holding out? And the wood? Tell Bascom to bring what you need and I'll O.K. the bill."

No. Things had changed, now that the town was growing. There had been a lot of talk about business inefficiency, and younger men were in office now. Business men who talked crisply of bonded indebtedness, assets and liabilities, overhead, and mendicancy; words that Lem may have understood but never thought of using.

Old George gave Tommy his forkful of hay. There was enough of that to last a while, thank the Lord. He wouldn't have to ask for so much after all. Just some oats for Tommy and maybe a bag of flour and a little salt pork for himself. He could get along on that all right.

He went into the stall and slapped Tommy's sleek rump. "Get over there, you old bag of bones, and let me clean out here," he said and Tommy stopped eating and nuzzled him playfully with a questing, soft, upper lip.

"What's the idea?" Old George wanted to know. "You

expect to get sugar every time I come near you? Eat your oats and stop pushin' me around, can't you? This place looks like it hadn't been cleaned for a week."

So Tommy ate his oats and half the hay while Old George removed the straw bedding and spread it out of doors in the sun and then swept and sanded the stall floor.

"There, doggone ya," he said then. "You're more bother than your homely hide is worth. I've a good mind to lick the tar out of you. Want me to?"

Tommy shook his head in a vigorous negative.

"You don't, eh? Well, will you be good if I don't?"

Tommy nodded an equally vigorous affirmative.

"Well, all right then," grumbled Old George. "I'll let you off this time. I'm goin' in now to make a cup of coffee but if I hear you raising Cain out here I'll come and give you something you won't forget in a hurry. Do you understand that?"

Tommy admitted that he understood. Old George gave him a parting slap and hobbled back through the shed and paused at the kitchen door. He waited there, as always, for a moment and Tommy whinnied softly. Then Old George went in and closed the door.

The tea kettle was boiling briskly. The coffee can, like the oat barrel, was nearly empty but a scant teaspoonful made one fairly strong cup. Once there had been plenty of sugar and cream for it, but not of late years. There was no place in business for an old man who was crippled with rheumatism. It had been eight—no—nine years, since the foreman had told him he had better lay off for a while and doctor up. He had hated worst of all to leave the lathe for someone else to run. They might neglect to oil the head properly or crowd the centers too tight, or something. Things looked so shiny in the lathe, after you had checked up with the "mike" and emery clothed them. Steel came out burnished silver and brass was the purest gold. But a man needed sensitive, steady fingers to feel out a size with the micrometer, and the fingers on Old George's hand had grown steadily worse. The knuckles were enlarged now. The worn gold band that Mary had given him would never come off again. The fingers that once had been long and shapely and cunning were so crooked now that he opened them with difficulty—and then they were far from straight.

Oh, well. Old George sighed and sipped his coffee. The toast was dry and tasteless, without butter, but he ate it without noticing the lack of flavor. He was thinking about Tommy's oats.

"I'll go down and see Mr. Stone this morning," he decided as he wiped his coffee cup and put the kitchen in order. "Just as soon as I straighten out here and get Tommy fixed up I'll go down and see him."

He didn't though. He had just finished polishing the stove when there came an aggressive rap on the little side door. Old George hobbled across the floor, polishing cloth in hand, and opened it. Mr. Stone stood in the doorway.

Mr. Stone was forty. His sleek black hair was already greying at the temples but his carriage was that of a youth of twenty. He surveyed Old George through eyes set a trifle too close together. Eyes that, behind their double lenses, looked as cold and impassive as those of a dead fish.

"Good morning, Mr. Stone. Won't you come in and have a seat?" For some unknown reason Old George was feeling ill at ease. "I was thinking about you this morning."

"And I've been thinking about you for several days." Mr. Stone's words were close clipped and his tone incisive. "The board has reached a decision at last concerning those dependent upon it for support. Paupers, to speak plainly. The old matter of individual maintenance has been a subject of controversy among us for some weeks but we came to an agreement several days ago. I am glad to be able to say that the board has adopted the plan I presented. In the future our paupers will be handled collectively, which is a better, cheaper and more satisfactory arrangement."

Old George blinked. "I guess I don't quite get what you're drivin' at, Mr. Stone," he said. "Some change you're thinkin' of makin'?"

"Exactly," Mr. Stone informed him coldly. "Tomorrow at twelve I'll have a car here to take you to the County Farm. Try and have what articles of clothing you may own packed before that time. You may also take any small personal belongings to which you may have become attached, but nothing not easily moved. Try and be ready at twelve."

"You mean—" Old George's voice quavered. He swallowed and tried again. "You mean you're goin' to take me away from my—home? Why, Mr. Stone, I've lived here ever since I was married. I—I couldn't get used to any other place."

"Oh, yes you can," Mr. Stone explained condescendingly. "You will have a warm room, a comfortable bed and three meals a day. Nothing to worry about and nothing at all to do. You will be quite happy there, I am sure."

"But this house—it means a lot to me, Mr. Stone. Bud was born here. I was thinkin' this mornin' about that. And Mary—Mary died in that room, there. It's a home you're askin' me to leave."

"I understand how you feel," said Mr. Stone. "I understand perfectly. But a few days in pleasant surroundings, among congenial companions, and you will have forgotten all this."

"Couldn't they—don't you suppose we could raise a little more money on the place? Wouldn't the bank—"

"Impossible," snapped the chairman of the board. "You know it is impossible. The bank has every cent invested here they care to risk. They would have foreclosed long ago if the town had not paid the interest on the loans. Absolutely impossible."

Old George glanced slowly about the room. The morning sun shone fiercely upon the ebony stove. The kettle glittered bravely and the copper over the kitchen sink glowed luminously. He sighed, and then, as a new thought flashed in his brain, he asked quickly, "Could I—do you suppose they've got a box stall for Tommy? He's not used to being tied up."

"I have made arrangements about the horse," Mr. Stone informed him and Old George's careworn face lighted up in a sudden, happy smile.

"Oh, thanks, Mr. Stone. That's awfully good of you. You see Tommy—"

"I have arranged," said Mr. Stone, "to place the horse with Lamson, the butcher. He is willing to pay fifty dollars for him and that will just about take care of the interest now due on the mortgage. He will get him tomorrow, after you have gone."

"You mean you have sold Tommy? Tommy? They're going to use Tommy to haul a butcher's cart?" Old George's voice rose in an indignant crescendo. "Why

Tommy's a saddle horse. He's never been harnessed. He's a thoroughbred, Mr. Stone, a thoroughbred."

"He's just a horse, however," said Mr. Stone, "and I consider the town fortunate to get a fifty dollar offer for him. There is no place on the County Farm for a saddle horse. No, absolutely none. Sorry, of course, but that is final." He strode to the door. "Until tomorrow, then. Be ready at twelve sharp. Don't forget."

He went out and closed the door.

Old George sat for many long minutes, scarcely breathing. Then he got up slowly and hobbled out to the stable and into Tommy's stall. He groped blindly up the horse's withers until his trembling arm encircled the satin neck.

Then a pair of quarrelsome sparrows, upon the roof of the old barn, ceased their bickering, momentarily, to listen to the unaccustomed sound of a broken-hearted old man crying pitifully in a horse's silken mane.

Later, Old George said, "It isn't myself I'm thinkin' about, Tommy. I'm tough and I can stand most anything —but it—it don't seem hardly fair for 'em to sell you."

Still later he said, "I'm goin' to leave it to you, Tommy. Do you want to haul a butcher's cart around town the rest of your life? Do you?"

Tommy looked bewildered and nuzzled his master's pockets but Old George pushed him away.

"Do you?"

Tommy tossed his head and gave it that emphatic, negative shake.

"All right, Tommy." Old George's voice was quite steady now. "I'll fix things so you won't have to. I'll fix everything all right, Tommy. Nobody's goin' to hurt *you*."

The five tinny notes of the clock aroused Old George the next morning. He moved slightly, and moaned feebly. This was not an awakening but rather a gradual recurrence of life to his numbed senses. His body was wracked with pain, for yesterday he had plumbed the depths of physical exhaustion. He had not slept. Through the long night phantoms had hovered around his bedside and half forgotten faces lived again in his fevered imagination.

It was hard, now, to separate the real from the imaginary but, bit by bit, he remembered. Then he thought of Tommy, and at once reason returned. Tommy, and work yet to be done. Tortured body and aching limbs could not stop him now. Old George got up.

The oat barrel was emptied in Tommy's feed box that morning. There were almost five quarts. After that he had two carrots, five medium-sized potatoes and half a loaf of bread that was just a trifle stale. He would have had more but that emptied the larder. Not that it made any difference. Old George had no appetite this morning.

He sat on a low stool and watched the horse finish his forkful of hay. Then he hobbled to the kitchen and returned presently with a pail of water. Tommy drank that, asked for more and got it.

Then the old man groomed him. From forelock to fetlock, with curry comb and brush, he received the outstanding grooming of his well-groomed life. After that Old George went over him meticulously with a soft cloth and, at the end, he glistened like a fur seal.

Then, when the last minute speck of dust had been wiped away, Old George folded the dust cloth and packed it carefully in the little cupboard where Tommy's things were kept, after which he hobbled once more to the house. He returned shortly, clad in an ill fitting old coat that hung limply about his emaciated frame but bulged strangely at the waist.

He opened the stable door, said, "Come on Tommy," and led the way across the stable, out through the open door, across the weed grown driveway, around to the rear of the barn.

With his nose ever and anon touching the shoulder or neck of the old man, Tommy followed, stepping high and lightly, the morning sun striking splashes of silver across his chestnut coat. His mane rippled in a vagrant breeze and the horse lifted his head high and shook it.

Out behind the barn Old George stopped and, without command, Tommy stopped also. There was a smell of new earth in the air. There was a big pile of it over there. He sniffed at the yawning hole at his feet. Sniffed disdainfully. He could vault that as lightly as any deer and, in the next stride, take the high old fence beyond. Many a time he—

"Well, old son, you've been a good horse," Old George was saying, and Tommy pricked his ears to listen. "We've had a lot of fun together, you and I, but I guess that's all over now. I didn't tell you yesterday, Tommy, I couldn't; but they're takin' me down to the County Farm at noon today. I don't want to go. I—I wanted to stay here, with you. Why couldn't they have let us? It would have only been a few years more. There isn't any way out, son, for me. I've got to go. But I couldn't let them have you, Tommy, to abuse and bang around. That's why I'm doin' this. You understand. Don't you Tommy?"

Tommy nodded yes.

"I knew you would." Old George's arm was around his neck now. "I'll put your blanket around you, Tommy. I wish I could buy you a new one but—I can't." A gnarled and knotted old hand stroked Tommy's ears and parted the flaxen forelock. "And Tommy! There was a little oak growin' here. I saved it. I'll plant it here—afterwards—for you, Tommy. That's all I can do." The unsightly old fingers, that clung to the crinkly forelock, trembled like those of a palsied man.

Now that the time had come for the last, supreme effort, could he do it? Could his poor old brain control those unruly hands in their last work of love. He fumbled beneath the ragged coat until his trembling fingers closed around the butt of the Colt that had ridden with him up from the Rio Grande. Then he knew. The shiny old gun lay in a misshapen old hand that was as steady as a rock.

"You'll forgive me, won't you, Tommy?"

"Yes."

Old George took three backward steps. Tommy, watching, lifted his head high and tossed his flowing mane.

"Hold your head down, Tommy."

From the fence a sleepy robin flashed into sudden flight as the startled echoes leaped out in the morning stillness—crashed, far flung, against the distant wood, and whispered into nothingness.

Old George buttoned his well brushed coat about his spare form and sank down in the chair by which his packed bag stood. His weary old eyes wandered about the room. The stove shone bravely. The pine floor, drying from its recent scrubbing, gleamed white. The old copper glowed softly. Everything was—

THOROUGHBRED

The little old clock on the mantel clicked warningly, then, after a moment, struck twelve tinny notes.

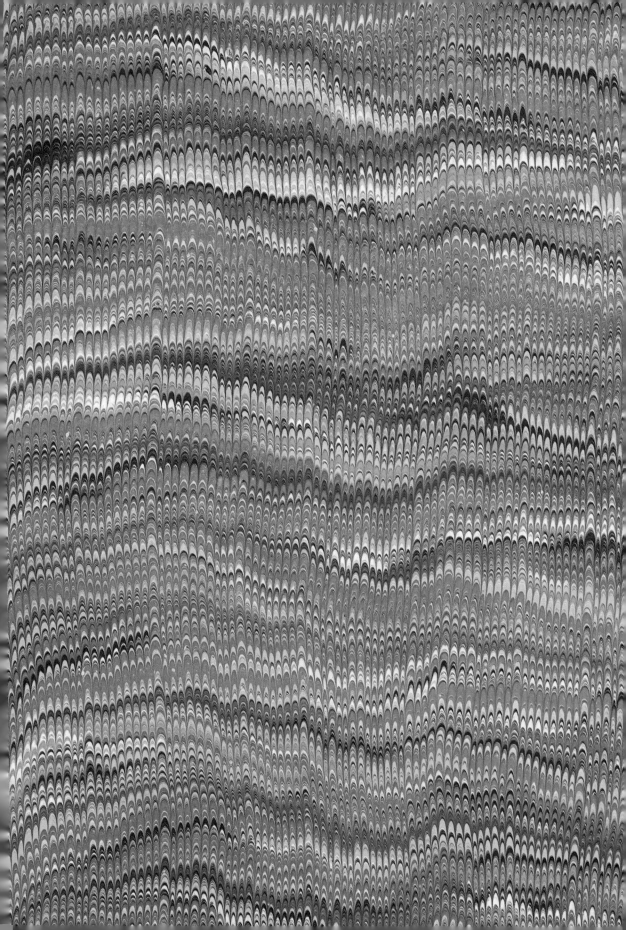